THE ST. THOMAS MORE LECTURES, 1

Sponsored by the

St. Thomas More House, Yale University

THE PROBLEM OF GOD

YESTERDAY AND TODAY

by John Courtney Murray, S.J.

NEW HAVEN AND LONDON, YALE UNIVERSITY PRESS

Designed by Crimilda Pontes,
set in Garamond type,
and printed in the United States of America by
BookCrafters, Inc.,
Chelsea, Michigan.

Library of Congress catalog card number: 63–13970
ISBN: 0–300–00781–7 (cloth),
       0–300–00171–1 (paper)

33   32   31   30   29   28   27

NIHIL OBSTAT: Rev. Carroll E. Satterfield, *Censor Librorum*

IMPRIMATUR: ✠ Most Rev. Lawrence J. Shehan, D.D.,
Archbishop of Baltimore
November 6, 1963

IMPRIMI POTEST: John J. McGinty, S.J.
September 15, 1962

···❧❦❧ PREFACE ❦❧❦···

IN THE WINTER of 1962 it was my privilege to give the inaugural series of St. Thomas More Lectures at Yale University. I spoke from notes, since I was largely drawing on materials and ideas familiar from detailed use in my courses in theology at Woodstock College. In preparing the lectures for publication, I thought it best to be faithful to the sense and style of the original notes, insofar as they had either style or sense. The decisive reason was that it seemed important to keep the story-line clean, to keep it moving, and to resist the temptation to blur it by development of particular episodes and ideas or halt it by pausing to append citation. In the lectures, I did not undertake to do more than present the line of a story which is also the structure of an argument. These pages will have served their purpose if they furnish anyone with the framework for further study of the story with a view to a fuller understanding of history's most momentous argument.

My affection for the Yale community, faculty and students,

dates principally from the year 1951–52 which I spent as visiting professor in the department of philosophy. The affection has been strengthened and further informed with a sense of gratitude by the invitation of the University to give the St. Thomas More Lectures and by the response of the community to their presentation. I must also record my gratitude to the Yale University Press for having undertaken their publication.

J. C. M.

Woodstock, Maryland
June 1963

⸺⧉[CONTENTS]⧉⸺

INTRODUCTION

THE PHRASE "the problem of God" is distinctively modern. Its currency, if not its coinage, seems to derive from Edouard Le Roy's book *Le Problème de Dieu*, published in 1929. No one reads the book today, but it aroused a good deal of discussion in its time. It belongs to the last phase of the modernist crisis, so-called, a crisis of the philosophical and historical intelligence as well as of religious faith. Hence, the phrase has a characteristic ring to our ears, upon which the correspondent phrases, "the God of reason" and "the Christ of history," strike discordantly as contradictions *in adiecto*. Whatever the resonances of the phrase, the problem itself is as old as the oldest traditions of the Bible. Only within the biblical tradition is God exhibited so as to give rise to a problem in the mind of man. Only within this tradition as it has been historically wedded to Western culture has the mind of man been so tutored that it has come to grasp the God of the Bible as a problem.

1

The problem is with us as it was with our forebears, and, if we are to understand today's problem in depth, it will be necessary to review the problem of yesterday. By yesterday I mean nothing less than the great span of time that stretches back to a date somewhere between 1250 and 1230 B.C., the conjectural date of the exodus of the Hebrew people from Egypt. The problem appeared in Israel in the formative days of the People of God. It presented itself in the form of two pairs of questions, as we shall see. It reappeared in the New Testament where its basic Old Testament structure was not radically altered but where, in consequence of the event of Christ, its substance acquired all the newness of the New Testament itself. In both Testaments the problem was that of the presence of God: is he the "living" God in the biblical sense? More generally, it was, as it still is, the problem of God as it arises on the level of the religious existence. This is the subject of my first lecture.

The second epoch of yesterday begins in the patristic age. Then, in consequence of the new issues raised in the Arian and Eunomian controversies, the biblical problem of God was transposed to a different level of discourse, the level of theological understanding. It came to be posited no longer simply in intersubjective and descriptive terms but in ontological and definitive terms. The new problem was, first, the relationship of the Logos-Son to the Father, and, second, the knowledge of and names of God.

The great Fathers of the Church dealt with the new theological problems only inchoately. Certain definitive positions were established, but they served only to launch further inquiry, which came to term in the systematization of St. Thomas Aquinas. This whole development is the subject of my second lecture.

The problem of God has its obverse in the problem of the

godless man. Only in recent times has he become a phenomenon of major magnitude and a determinant factor in the world of intellect, popular culture, and politics. But he has his antecedents in biblical times. In my third lecture, after a brief look at the three types of the godless man exhibited in the Bible, I shall attempt a theological description and evaluation of the different forms of atheism characteristic of the modern and the post-modern worlds. The subtitle of this third lecture, "The Death of God," seems appropriate, since the appearance of Nietzsche's famous myth may be fairly regarded as marking the break between the modern and the post-modern phases of the problem of the godless man. I use the word *myth* in its precise sense. The death of God is not a fact; it never happened. But men have projected the idea, as a fact, into history in an effort to account for an aspect of the human condition and for a direction of human striving in what has been called the "age of the absence of God."

A word is required here about my purpose and method. My purpose is neither apologetic nor polemic, though some controversial statements will doubtless be made. My purpose is not to prove anything, much less to persuade anybody. I do not undertake to confute or even to dispute, and certainly I shall not exhort. My purpose is to set forth a theological understanding of the problem of God as it has appeared in successive historical phases. In consequence, the method will be descriptive and historical.

It is hardly necessary to add that, given the great breadth of my canvas, it is not to be expected that I shall play the scholarly mandarin, drawing delicately with an exquisite Chinese brush. I am not unaware of Lord Acton's strictures on the use of the "big brush" in matters historical. Nevertheless, I must use it, hoping at least not to be slovenly in its use.

This introduction to my subject should include a comment on the uniqueness of the problem of God amid the whole range of problems that man faces. If God is a reality, his reality is unique; it will therefore present to man a unique problem. The problem of God exhibits only the barest analogy with the standard model of a problem as it is found in science. In the scientific world of observation and inference, hypothesis and verification, the data are, as it were, "out there." The scientist is distant and detached from them; other things being equal, any number of men who are scientists can do the same experiment and record the same results. No personal issues arise in the scientific problem. In contrast, the problem of God is primary among the fateful human questions that, as Pascal said, "take us by the throat." The whole man—as intelligent and free, as a body, a psychic apparatus, and a soul—is profoundly engaged both in the position of the problem and its solution. In fact, he is in a real sense a datum of the problem itself, and his solution of it has personal consequences that touch every aspect of his conduct, character, and consciousness. Moreover, the problem of God is unique in that no man may say of it, "It is not my problem." Dostoievski's challenge is valid: "If God is not, everything is permitted." But the challenge needs to be amended to include, "except one thing." If God is not, no one is permitted to say or even think that he is, for this would be a monstrous deception of oneself and of others. It would be to cherish and propagate a pernicious illusion whose result would necessarily be the destruction of man. On the other hand, if God is, again one thing is not permitted. It is not permitted that any man should be ignorant of him, for this ignorance, too, would be the destruction of man. On both counts, therefore, no man may say that the problem of God is not his problem.

THE BIBLICAL PROBLEM:
THE PRESENCE OF GOD

OUR FIRST LINE OF INQUIRY, which concerns the Old Testament, will proceed in three steps. My assumption is that the books of the Old Testament record the events of a sacred history in and through which God revealed himself to the people whom he chose as his own, and also record the developing faith of the people in the God who so revealed himself. The first step in the inquiry will be an exegesis of Exodus 3:1–15, the towering text that tells the story of the theophany to Moses at the burning bush, the commission of Moses as leader of the people, and the revelation of the Name under which God is to be known to his people. This event and its sequels—the Exodus from Egypt, the theophanies at Sinai, the striking of the Alliance, and the giving of the Code—are the major events on which the faith of the people and their existence as a people were founded. The exegesis of this text, as completed in the second step of the inquiry by a brief theological analysis of its content, will furnish us with at least a sufficient basis for the third step, which is a work of discernment whose purpose is to grasp the structure and content of the problem of God in the Old Testament.

The text and its context are known to everyone who has attended classes in Bible history. The descendants of the patriarchs are in Egypt, miserable under a system of forced labor. The young Moses is a shepherd of his father-in-law Jethro, in the land of Midian. One day near Mount Horeb God appears to him "under the form of a flame springing up out of a bush." Moses draws near in astonishment and curiosity, and a dialogue ensues. God announces his intention to "come down" to rescue his people from their bondage, and he lays a charge on Moses to be his emissary to Pharaoh and the agent of his people's deliverance. Moses protests his inadequacy: "Who am I . . . ?" He receives in return the divine promise: "I shall be with you." Still reluctant and fearful, Moses asks a further question: "Then Moses said to God: 'So be it. I go to the children of Israel and I say to them: "The God of your fathers has sent me to you." But if they ask me what his name is, what answer shall I give them?' Then God said to Moses: ' *'ehyeh* *ʾᵃšer* *'ehyeh.*' And he added: 'Thus you shall address yourself to the children of Israel: " *'ehyeh* has sent me to you." ' God further said to Moses: 'Thus you shall speak to the children of Israel: "Yahweh, the God of your fathers, the God of Abraham, the God of Isaac, and the God of Jacob has sent me to you." This is the name that I shall forever bear, and under this name future generations shall invoke me.' " The Hebrew phrase is an example of paronomasia, a play on words; in it Moses and the people were to catch the sense of the divine Name and to utter it in the sacred tetragrammaton, YHWH, Yahweh.

The name of a person in Hebrew thought was not a mere appellation used only for purposes of designation. The name was, as it were, the definition of the person. Even more, it was the person himself in the form of an alter ego which represented him, exhibited him, was him. To know the name of another was to know who and what the other was—his identity, qualities, and character, or, perhaps more exactly (since these are terms of static connotation, unfamiliar to the primitive mind), his power, role, function—what the other was entitled or empowered to do. To be "nameless" is to be "worthless" (Job 30:8), of no avail. "As his name is, so is he; 'Fool' is his name" (1 Samuel 25:25). In the case of God, the Hebrew impulse was not to know his existence or essence; these were alien concepts. It was to know his Name, which was an operative entity in its own right. Knowledge of God's Name was empowering: one could address him as God, call on him, enter into community with him, make valid claims upon him. Similarly, for the people to have the Name of God "put" upon them was to come into God's possession and under his protection: "Thou art in our midst, Yahweh; and we bear thy Name. Abandon us not" (Jeremiah 14:9).

Moses' request to know God's Name was therefore of high import. The problem is the interpretation of the enigmatic answer. There is a vast literature on the text, but we need not be concerned here with all the details of the argument which has gone on for so long among scholars. Only one philological certainty seems to be available, namely, that the divine answer to Moses' question bears in some sense on the "is-ness" of God. The word on which the text plays is an archaic form of the verb that means somehow "to be." For the rest, the issue is not philological certainty but adequate exegetical understanding of the text in its situation within the full faith of the Israelites. The question is, what did the people hear as they listened to the oral recitation or, later, to the reading of the story of Moses' decisive encounter with God? They listened with the inner ear of their religious faith to God's utterance of his Name. What they thus heard was what was in the mind of the Mosaic author. The ancient singers, the later editor, and those who listened to both all stood within one community and shared one mind. Today, therefore, our task is to read out of the text what the people of old heard in the text. There are three major possibilities.

The first is the most familiar to readers of the classical English versions of the Bible, Protestant and Catholic: "I am who I am." God affirms himself to be the Absolutely Existent One to whose being there is no limit or restriction. His very Name is Being, as the false gods and idols are nullities, nothingnesses, and therefore nameless. This sense is valid and true; it is in the text. But it was probably heard only later when the Hebrew ear had become attuned to metaphysical resonances through contact with Hellenistic culture. Then it appeared in the Septuagint (Greek) version: "I am he who is." One would risk anachronism if one were to read this sense back into the situation described in Exodus 3. It is not likely that this would be the sense caught by the ear of the primitive people of whom Moses was to take command. To them God was by definition the Power. Their concern was to know not his nature but his role in their community and his mode of action in their history. Moses' question was not a calm inquiry into the inherent attributes of the divine being; anxiously, he wanted to know God's operative attitudes toward himself and toward the people. I shall therefore put aside this exegesis.

The second interpretation takes the verb in a causative sense: "I make to be whatever comes to be." This sense has good philological warrant and would not be historically anachronistic. The belief that God is the Maker of All was present among the Israelites from the beginning. In fact, in all primitive religions the belief prevailed that the god stood at the origin of the world. It may, however, be doubted that the original hearers of the divine Name caught this cosmological sense in it. To them, Yahweh was in the first instance the God of their fathers, who created the people, who was Lord of the people, the Power behind their history. Only in the second instance was he the God of nature who created the heavens and the earth, who was the Power behind the processes of the material world. The Hebrew mentality inverted our perspective, in which God's activity as Creator has primacy over his redemptive activity as Savior. Therefore, I do not favor this exegesis.

There is a third interpretation which I consider more satisfactory because it yields a more adequate exegetical understanding. It asserts that, in the enigmatic play on words and in the Name Yahweh that embodies its sense, Moses and his people heard not the affirmation that God is or that he is Creator but the promise that he would be present with his people. God's utterance of his Name is to be understood in the light of the promise to Moses that precedes it ("I will be with you") and which in another form follows it: "I will help you to speak and I will tell you what you have to say" (4:12). The sense of the verb "to be" is relational, or intersubjective. For the ancient Israelites, as for all primitive peoples, existence was an affair of community; to be was to be-with-the-others. Existence was also an effective affair; to be was to be-in-action. Finally, existence was of the phenomenal, not the essential, order; to be was to be-there, concretely and in evidence. This primitive sense, which is nonetheless valid for being primitive, has come to the fore again in current existential philosophies —for instance, in the technical German word *Dasein* as contrasted with *Sein*.

In uttering his Name, God says, "I shall be there, with you, in power" (*'ehyeh*). One of the multitudinous echoes of this sense which sound all through the Old Testament was uttered on the eve of the restoration of the kingdom of Judah when Deutero-Isaiah prophesied: "Therefore my people shall know my name; therefore in that day they shall know that it is I who says: 'Here I am' " (Isaiah 52:6).

There remains the relative clause, " *'ašer 'ehyeh*," which plays on the verb. One might perhaps consider that it merely adds emphasis to the promise: "Indeed, in all reality, I shall be there, with you." But a more adequate exegesis would be to take the clause as a suggestion of the aura of the numinous that envelops the presence of God, an aura that emanates from the divine Name itself. Thus, by its very enigmatic character, the total phrase opens awe-inspiring perspectives on the mystery that lies behind the promise to Moses and the people. To capture this full suggestion and to keep the paronomastic cadence of the original Hebrew, one might translate: "I shall be there as who I am shall I be there."

This exegesis needs to be completed by a brief theological analysis. The text, thus understood, contains a threefold revelation—of God's immanence in history, of his transcendence to history, and of his transparence through history. God first asserts the fact of his presence in the history of his people: "I shall be there." Second, he asserts the mystery of his own being: "I shall be there as who I am." His mystery is a mode of absence. Third, he asserts that, despite his absence in mystery, he will make himself known to his people: "As who I am shall I be there." The mode of his transparence is through his action, through the saving events of the sacred history of Israel. However, what thus becomes known is only his saving will. He himself, in his being and nature, remains forever unknown to men, hidden from them. I should like briefly to develop this threefold significance of the divine Name revealed in our text.

"I shall be there, actively, with you." The initial revelation is of God's will to "come down" to rescue his people. The mode of expression in verse 8 is anthropomorphic, but the anthropomorphism, here as elsewhere in the Old Testament, serves to emphasize the reality of God's intervention in history. Moreover, the verbal form in verse 14 has a frequentative sense: "I shall be with you time and again, in many 'visitations.' " It also has the connotations of becoming, or perhaps even befalling, rather than simply of being. God does not indeed become God, but, in the successive junctures of history, in the new situations that continually befall, God becomes God-with-his-people. Finally, as the verbal form asserts the contingency of the divine presence, it also implies its continuity. Over against the inconstancy and infidelity of the people, who continually absent themselves from God, the Name Yahweh affirms the constancy of God, his unchangeable fidelity to his promise of presence. Malachi, the last of the prophets, stated this first facet of the primitive revelation: "I [am] Yahweh; I do not change" (3:6).

Understood as affirming the faithful presence of God among his people, the Name Yahweh is the "banner" of Israel (Exodus 17:15), the rallying standard about which the tribes realize their religious and national unity as a people. In this sense the divine Name is at the root of the whole theology of the people of Yahweh that develops throughout the Old Testament. In particular, it inspires the concept of the people of God as a qualitative concept, religious, not ethnic. This view becomes explicit chiefly in Ezechiel, though it is suggested in the earliest traditions of the Pentateuch. Only they are the true people of God who dwell with him as he dwells with them, who "go with" Yahweh as he "goes with" them.

"I shall be there as who I am." Here the perspectives of meaning lengthen into two reaches of mystery. There is first the mystery of the sovereign freedom with which God presents himself to the people. The initiative of the presentation rests with him; he "comes down" but not as though summoned. The religion of the Old Testament is utterly free of any magical element. Yahweh asserts his power by his own free choice. He cannot be controlled by magical constraints. He does not deliver himself into the power of men or permit men to dispose of his power. Moreover, although the Old Testament revelation bears, if you will, on the function of God in history, Yahweh is not the functional God of contemporary immanentist theory and its theologically decadent taste—a God whose function is to respond to man's religious needs and satisfy his spiritual aspirations. In the final analysis, Yahweh is not present to meet the needs of men or to fulfill their aspirations or, even, to terminate their quest for something beyond themselves. Yahweh does not intervene in history or enter the human situation as if he were in any way required by history or by the situation. God comes down to men in their misery always as he came down to Moses in Midian, "to the westward part of the desert." He comes down with all the mystery that attaches to the concept of freedom when freedom is stretched to infinity—to the point where it breaks through the limits of the conceptual, goes beyond the manner of understanding that conception may bring, and passes into the far regions of utter ineffability. Precisely in the mysterious freedom of his presence Yahweh is manifested as the Lord, the one Lord of his own action, who does not abide man's questions because he stands beyond all questioning. In giving himself the Name Yahweh, God forestalls the question that is somehow native to the heart of man,

"Why are you here?" or, in its more usual form, "Why are you not here?" The answer, which refuses the question in both its forms, is: "I shall be there as who I am."

(Incidentally, the affirmation of the divine freedom made in the Name Yahweh is linked to two related Old Testament themes—the election of Israel and the alliance of Yahweh with Israel as his chosen people. Together they have given rise to the "scandal of particularity," so-called. Through all the sweep of space, in all the course of time, along the whole train of humanity, why is God present here and not there, now and not then, to this nation or man and not to others? There is indeed a scandal for intelligence here. But this subject is not mine.)

Beyond the mystery of the divine freedom asserted in the divine Name, there lies the mystery of God as he is in himself. This, too, is suggested in the giving of the Name. The text has been interpreted by some exegetes as a refusal of Moses' question. "I am who I am," that is to say, "I will not tell you my name." The parallel is drawn with the story in the Book of Judges in which the birth of Samson is foretold to Manoah and his wife by "the angel of Yahweh" (this is the customary Old Testament circumlocution for Yahweh himself in his somehow visible visitations to men). Manoah, the story goes, "did not know that he was the angel of Yahweh." Hence he puts the question: "What is your name, that we may honor you when your word comes true?" And Yahweh said to him, "Why do you ask for my name? It is ineffable" (Judges 14:17–18). Similarly, some scholars say God's answer to Moses is a refusal to answer. As a total exegesis this will hardly do, but it contains a profound truth. God does not disclose his intimate Name, his proper identity as God. This is his own secret, not to be told to men because it could not possibly be understood by them. Only God knows who and what God is. The Name of God is ineffable.

This revelatory significance of the Name Yahweh was elaborated by Isaiah, and chiefly by Deutero-Isaiah, the anonymous prophet of the sixth century who has been called the "theologian of the divine Name." The favorite Isaian theme is Yahweh as the Holy One before whom, "sitting upon a throne high and uplifted," the seraphim veil themselves completely while they unendingly sing the trisagion: "Holy, holy, holy is the Lord of hosts" (6:1). The philosopher transforms this biblical theme into the thesis of the divine transcendence, and imagination expresses this latter concept spatially in terms of distance. As the Holy One, God is separated by the distance of an immeasurable height from the earth that he created. As the Holy One, God also is the First and the Last (Isaiah 48:12 et passim), who stands outside the whole stretch of time, untouched by its fatal corrosions. Moreover, as the Holy One, God is the Utterly Other, totally unlike his creation. "To whom could you liken me, and who would be my equal, says the Holy One" (40:25). This is the doctrine behind the prohibition, laid on Israel in Mosaic times, against all carved images of Yahweh (Exodus 20:4). There ensues the Isaian paradox, repeated in many texts: God is "the Holy One of Israel" (5:19). Infinitely distant from the people, he is "in their midst" (12:6). In their midst, he "hides himself" (45:15). What the Holy One is remains forever unknown. In the end, the people do not know his Name.

"As who I am shall I be there." On listening to the text the third time, one hears the promise that God, remaining unknown, will yet make himself known. He is present as the Power. Presence involves transparency; one sees through the veil of otherness into the other and knows his quality, intentions, attitudes. Thus, through his mighty works, God becomes transparent to his people. He is known to be present in faithful goodness—what the Hebrew untranslatably calls *ḥesed*—as the Power who alone can save and who graciously wills to save. If, however, the people are faithless, if they absent themselves from him, he makes his abiding presence felt in judgment on them. This theme of the twofold presence of Yahweh, which is firmly remarked in the Mosaic tradition, was later fully developed, chiefly by Ezechiel. The epoch of the Exile was for Israel the "age of the absence of God." But the lesson of all its forlornness was expressed by Ezechiel in his refrain: "So shall they know that I am Yahweh" (7:27). Faithful to his Name, he is still present, but in a wrath that is like an absence. There will, however, be a rescue and a return to the homeland, and its lesson will be the same: "They shall know that I am Yahweh, when I break the bars of their yoke and rescue them from the hand of those who enslaved them. . . . They shall know that I, Yahweh, their God, am with them, and that they, the house of Israel, are my people" (34:27, 30). In all his works, of judgment as of rescue, Yahweh becomes transparent, known to his people, who name him from their experience of his works. He whose one Name is ineffable is given the many names that are strewn over the pages of the Old Testament.

There are, for instance, the many names in the theophany on Mount Sinai: "Yahweh, Yahweh, a God merciful and gracious, slow to anger, abounding in steadfast love and faithfulness, keeping steadfast love to the thousandth generation, forgiving iniquity and transgression and sin, without leaving it unpunished . . ." (Exodus 34:6–7). The names appear as adjectives, designating qualities, but in their meaning with regard to God they are proper names, substantives that declare what God is. To be exact, they declare what God is only in a sense. These many names are of human mintage; they are taken from the language of men concerning men. They are used by men to name the God who becomes known in his mighty works in history, but they do not and cannot say what God is in himself. No one of them, and not the whole sum of them, makes known the unknowable, unutterable Name of God. They do, however, describe God's ways with men; they articulate his relation to his people; they portray his attitudes. Thus, the many names are really names of God at the same time as they leave God himself, in the end, unnamed. This is the best that human words, conceived in the mind of man, can hope to do. The only knowledge of God to which man can aspire is that which Moses prayed for in a text that has a marvelous theological exactitude however it is construed: "Now therefore I pray thee, if I have found favor with thee, show me thy ways, that so I may know thee" (Exodus 33:13). This is, in effect, a prayer for the fulfillment of the promise inherent in the Name Yahweh: "I shall be there as who I am shall I be there."

After this summary exegetical and theological analysis, we are sufficiently prepared, I think, for the third step in our inquiry. The question now concerns the structure and content of the problem of God as it arises in the Old Testament. Hitherto I have simply assembled some data with regard to what the Israelites heard on listening to the divine Name Yahweh. Is it possible to discern in these data what the problem of God was for the man of the Old Testament? I think it will be seen that the problem was complex. As it arose out of the religious situation described, it consisted of four questions or, better, of two pairs of questions, which interlock and overlap.

I shall call the four questions, in their order, existential and functional, noetic and onomastic.

The existential question is whether God is here with us now. The word "existential" bears a biblical sense, referring to the active existence of God in history, his presence in the midst of his people. The question appears frequently in the text of the Old Testament. It appears, for instance, in the story of the Exodus, after the incident at the place called Massah (the place of testing) and Meribah (the place of fault-finding) where water gushed from the rock when Moses struck it at God's command (Exodus 17:1–7). The people had found fault with Moses and with Yahweh himself because they were without water. They "put the Lord to the test" (17:2). The question in their minds was, "Is the Lord in our midst or not?" (17:7). The question was not speculative, academic, merely curious; it was fraught with a profound religious anxiety. The same anxious question reappears continually in Israelite history, with the sharpest urgency during the Exile of the sixth century. Had the sacred history come to an end? Was God now no longer with his people? This was the issue to which Deutero-Isaiah spoke with high poetic passion in the "Book of the Consolation of Israel," as chapters 40–55 of Isaiah have been called. The Holy One of Israel, he reiterates, is still in the midst of his people, and there will be a new Exodus, from Babylon as from Egypt: "At the head of the column Yahweh will march; and your rear guard will be the God of Israel" (52:12). When the tension of the anxiety in the existential question relaxed into religious doubt, the results were the repeated falls of Israel into idolatry. The driving impulse behind all idolatry is not simply to have a god, to have something to worship; it is to have the god here, now, accessible, visibly active, disponible. "Come, make us a god to go ahead of us," said the people to

Aaron (Exodus 32:1) in the absence of Moses (which was to them somehow also the absence of the God who had made Moses their leader). When they saw the golden bull, frequently the symbol of divinity in the ancient East, they cried: "Here is your god, O Israel!" (32:4). Finally, the living nerve of inner religious anxiety about the presence of God was touched by the taunt flung at the Israelites by the surrounding pagan nations. The challenge took the form of a question, not philosophical but existential in tenor; it bore not on God's being but, as it were, on his location in time and space. Mockingly, the nations asked: "Where is your God?" (Psalms 115:2). Is he with you or not? Is he active in your behalf or not? This was the first form of the post-modern question, "Is God dead?"

The second question is inseparable from the first. The God who is here with us—what is he? That is, what is he toward us? What is he here to do for us? This is the functional question. It has to do with the power of God, his action in history, his attitude toward the people with whom he is present.

This question underlies the elaborate orchestration of the theme to which reference has already been made—the twofold role of Yahweh, who is present among his people both as Savior and as Judge, in steadfast love and in wrath. The functional question also lies behind the long Old Testament polemic against idols, in a negative form. The polemic, which is often greatly sardonic, especially in Isaiah, deals with the crucial issue, what God is not. This is the first and all-important question to ask about God: what he is not. A mistake here means idolatry; hence the theme of the polemic is that God is not his creation. He is not to be identified with any of the forces of nature or the artifacts of man. These forces and artifacts have no divine function; there is no power of salvation in them.

Isaiah says of idols, "They are not—the whole lot of them. Their works are nothingness; air and emptiness, their carved images" (41:29).

The second pair of questions has to do with the order of knowledge and language. There is the noetic question: how is this God who is present as Savior and Judge to be known? Related to it is the onomastic question: how is this God, who is known to be present but also known to be God, to be named? These related questions underlie the prevailing Old Testament paradox, inherent in the divine Name Yahweh, which was sharpened by Deutero-Isaiah. The Name of God is ineffable; it is not given to men to know what God is. On the other hand, God has given himself to be known and named by men. We have seen the resolution of the paradox in Moses' prayer. God is known through his "ways," in the course of his "visitations" of his people. The two words are almost technical. The latter is used in Exodus 3:16 where Moses is bid to tell the elders of Israel that God had "visited" him. Its use is frequent elsewhere to express the historical interventions of God, whether in gracious rescue or in wrathful judgment. In and through these visitations, God is known. Hence the first answer to the noetic question is that the knowledge of God is mediated not by metaphysical reflection on the necessity of his being but by historical experience of his presence, which was not at all necessary but utterly contingent and most graciously free. Thus, God is known to be the "living" God. The epithet is constant and characteristic. It embodies the whole Israelite religious experience of Yahweh, the God of the fathers, who freely and graciously came down into the midst of the people, there to be the indwelling, energizing principle of their life as a people. It was this experience of the living God that was minted down into the humanly manageable coinage of the many names of God. Known as living, God was named from his manifold life-giving "ways" with his people.

The question of the knowledge and names of God has a later development, which is visible in the wisdom literature. Two factors seem to have prompted the development. The first was fuller reflection on the primitive faith in God as creator of the universe. The Hebrew mind moved back to this reflection from the dominant religious experience of God as the Lord of history. The second factor was Hebrew contact with Hellenistic culture and its more refined idolatries and sophisticated skepticism. Then rose the question of the testimony of the material world to God. In its Hebraic form, the question was whether the cosmos testifies to the fact that it is not itself divine. From the depths of the ancient faith there came up a resounding affirmation. The Israelite world-view was never touched by any taint of pantheism. However seductive to the philosopher, pantheism was no temptation to the people whose sense of God as the Holy One made pantheism unthinkable. Moreover, the Israelite world-view was purified of all sense of demonic inhabitation and control of the natural universe. Primitive mythologies were full of this sense of dark powers in nature, hostile to man as to deity. But the faith of Israel was cleansed of it by the lightsome sense of God as the one Lord. By the simple majesty of a word, uttered when he alone was "there," in the beginning, God, the First, facing nothingness, made the heavens and the earth. And his dominion over all the forces that dwell in the natural world was as absolute and unshared as his dominion over the destinies of the people whom he alone had also created, by his word of choice, out of the nothingness of a slavish existence in Egypt.

There was, however, a more subtle issue. Given that the

universe is not divine, is its reality wholly secular or is it also sacral? Does it so present itself as the work of God that the invisible Lord becomes somehow visible through it? Is nature, like history, a transparency, so that in its beauties and powers the higher majesty of its Artisan and Ruler is somehow apparent? The Hebrew answer is unhesitatingly affirmative. It furnishes the premise for the indictment, found in the Wisdom of Solomon 13:1–9, of the idolatrous intellectuals of Egyptian Alexandria and of all the Near East. So luminously evident does the answer seem to the Sage of Israel that, despite his sympathy for these men in their search for truth, he qualifies them as "thorough fools" (13:1) because of their failure to find "him who is" in the course of their scrutiny of "the good things that were visible."

I come now to the issue of the alternative responses to the problem of God in its Old Testament structure and substance. The alternatives are called "knowledge" of God and "ignorance" of God. These concepts, however, must be filled with their proper Old Testament content, which was far more dense than the thin meaning that attaches to the words as we customarily use them. For the Hebrew mind, to be is to be-with-the-others. So, also, to know the other is to commune with the other, actively to relate oneself to the other in a relationship that involves the whole self. Revealingly, the word is also used of sexual intercourse. Knowledge is not simply an affair of intelligence; it is an affair of the heart, in the biblical sense of the heart as the center and source of the whole inner life in its full complex of thought, desire, and moral decision.

In particular, the knowledge of God carries all these implications. The premise of the people's knowledge of God was the fact that God had first known them. His knowledge of them found active historical expression in all the *mirabilia Dei*, the wonderful works wherein God displayed his solicitude for them. The formula for this knowledge, in which the heart of God himself was engaged, was the prophetic refrain of Ezechiel: "I will make my abode among them, and I will be their God and they will be my people" (37:27). For the people to know God, therefore, is for them to reciprocate the mode of God's knowledge of them. Their knowledge is not simply the abstract affirmation that God exists. It finds its true expression in the biblical acclamation that is at once an affirmation and a choice, that "Yahweh is our God," the "God with us" (Isaiah 8:10). Thus Hosea exhorts the people: "Let us know, let us press on to know Yahweh" (6:3)—that is, let us realize his presence, choose him as our Lord, ally ourselves to his purposes, consent to the exigencies of his steadfast love, obey his majestic will, accept without question his judgments. The exhortation follows the prophetic complaint against the people: "The spirit of harlotry is active within them; they do not know Yahweh" (5:4). The harlotry was the worship of false gods, the denial of God's knowledge of his people, his communication of himself to them, his right to their exclusive love. The consequence of idolatry was moral corruption: "Yahweh has a quarrel with the inhabitants of the land. There is no faithfulness, no love, no knowledge of God in the land. There is perjury and lying, assassination and theft, adultery and violence, murder upon murder" (4:2). Empty ritual is no substitute for the fullness of true religion, which is the knowledge of God: "For it is faithful love that I want, not sacrifices; the knowledge of God, not burnt offerings" (6:6).

Acknowledgment rather than knowledge would be the word here. The knowledge of God is an affair not simply of cognition but of recognition. It has to do not only with propositions and the admission of their truth but also with freedom, decision, and choice. Moreover, the biblical knowledge of God, like the biblical existence of God, is historical-existential. To know God is to recognize that he is here, in the situation of the moment; it is to recognize his action in the situation whether it be a deed of rescue or of wrath, and it is to respond to his action by a turning to the Lord, a "going with" him.

In turn, the biblical concept of ignorance of God is not a simple defect in the order of intelligence, a sheer lack of information. To be ignorant of God implies an active ignoring of him, a refusal to recognize him as present in the moment. It, too, is an affair of freedom, decision, and choice. I shall return to this subject when I come to the problem of the godless man.

Perhaps I have said enough to fulfill my intention, which was to illustrate the proposition that the Old Testament problem of God was constituted by two interrelated pairs of interpenetrating questions in all of which the issue of the presence of God is raised. The questions are asked in the intersubjective, not the metaphysical, mode of conception. That is to say, the problem directly concerns the Emmanuel of Isaiah, "God-with-us"; it does not directly concern God as he is in himself, the God-whose-essence-is-to-exist of a later theology. In other words the problem is posed on the plane of the religious existence, not on the plane of philosophical-theological inquiry. The matrix of the questions is the historical present. Therefore the questions themselves are concrete; they are questions of the moment. They are, in consequence, instant, urgent, and momentous in the full sense. The issues they raise are presented not simply for understanding but for decision. The questions oblige man not only to rise to the heights of intelligence where affirmations are made but also to descend to the depths of his own freedom where decisions are formed. The Old Testament problem of God, as the problem of his presence, is not offered for solution but for resolution. The alternate resolutions are in terms of knowledge of God and ignorance of God, in the sense explained. The confrontation in the questions is with the *living* God, and the issue, in the end, is life or death.

Some emphasis must be laid on the origins of the quadriform problematic, on the situation out of which the four questions rise—whether God is here-with-us, what God is doing here for us, how we are to know the God-with-us, and how we are to name him. Evidently, it was God himself who constituted the problematic by creating the situation. He came down in gracious freedom, and he confronts man on the plane of human historical existence. It is this fact which raises the four questions in their biblical form. They do not form a rational heuristic scheme devised by man on the basis of his common experience of himself, of others, of the world, and of himself-with-the-others-in-the-world. They are not, in other words, the fruit of philosophical reflection. The problematic is a datum of history, not a discovery of reason. The four questions themselves came down, as Yahweh himself came down. It would be idle to ask them in their biblical form on any other than the biblical basis, which is the mysterious story inherent in the divine Name Yahweh: "I shall be there as who I am shall I be there." This Name was not a human invention, as men might call God the Unconditioned, or the Absolute, or the Power beyond ourselves, or the One, or whatever else. The Name Yahweh was a divine revelation. By the giving of it God himself put to men the problem of God in a form that reason, left to itself, could never have devised. In fact, Hellenic reason found the problem in its biblical form quite scandalous. And reason remains Hellenic to this day.

I would further assert that, in its basic structure and in the central element of its substance, the Old Testament problematic endures as the permanent religious problematic of all mankind. The four questions remain valid for all time. Oddly enough, this proposition is implicitly recognized by the atheist school of contemporary existentialism. One may, if one wishes (so runs their thesis), assert that God is; the assertion is devoid of meaning because devoid of consequence. But one may not affirm that God exists, for existence means engagement in history, in a process of becoming, in all the risk of freedom. It cannot be permitted that God should so exist and also be God. The reasons for this thesis need not concern us here; we shall return to them later. At the moment the point is that this existentialist thesis itself attests, in an inverted way, the permanence of the biblical problem of God. For the biblical problem is precisely whether God so exists—whether he is engaged in history, in a process of becoming God-with-us at the risk of a clash with an opposing human freedom.

The New Testament

The New Testament raises the same question in a new way. The Christian views the New Testament as the fulfillment of the Old Testament but a fulfillment that is transcendent. The two Testaments are radically discontinuous, but, at the same time, there is a unity between them, whose main thread is the common theme of the divine presence, the active existence of God with his people. I shall narrow this vast subject to two interrelated points that are essential to my theme. First, the problem of God in the New Testament is identical in its quadriform structure with the Old Testament problem. Second, the substance of the New Testament problem is transcendently new, as new as the Name of God that was revealed in Christ.

The New Testament transforms the ancient problem of Yahweh into the new problem of Jesus. I do not use the latter phrase in the sense of the nineteenth-century Higher Criticism, for which the problem of Jesus centered on the issue whether the "historical Jesus" could be uncovered by the techniques and methods of historical research developed in the field of secular history, chiefly under the leadership of Von Ranke. We are not here concerned with the question of historical critique. It has, in any event, been largely outmoded by a happy enlargement of the conception of history and a consequent refinement of the notion of historical method. My assumption here is parallel to the assumption made in the case of the Old Testament. I assume that the New Testament records the faith of the early Christian community and that this faith was based on the new revelation contained in the total event of Christ.

From this point of view, the problem of Jesus is seen to have been stated by Jesus himself in the decisive query reported in all three Synoptic Evangelists; "Who am I, in your view of me?" (Mark 8:29). The question is cast in the intersubjective mode, in the existential terms familiar from the Old Testament: I, who am here with you in this moment—who am I, and what am I to you? Am I the Messiah of whom the Scriptures spoke? If this title defines my function, what, further, is my Name? Am I the Son, entitled by equality of power with God to bear the divine Name? Thus, the problem of God, in its New Testament form as the problem of Jesus, again centers on the presence of God in history, on his active existence with his people. The quadriform structure of the problematic is again discernible, though the substance of the four questions is radically new. There is the existential question whether, in the presence of the man Christ Jesus, God himself is present to his people. There is the inseparable functional

26

question of the role and office of Jesus the Christ. And the noetic and onomastic questions follow: how is God now to be known, and how is he to be named?

The ancient questions, in their new form, lie behind the answer given to them in the acclamation of the early Christian community: "Lord Jesus!" This is the Christian paraphrase of the Old Testament address to God as Yahweh, Emmanuel, God-with-us. Jesus bears the divine Name. He is Kyrios (the Greek translation, in the Septuagint, of the Hebrew Name Yahweh). He is the Lord, our Lord, the Lord-of-us. This affirmation and the questions latent in it form the burden of the primitive Christian kerygma (the Greek word for the apostolic preaching) of which the Acts of the Apostles preserve many examples. In St. Paul and St. John, this primitive preaching, which is a simple announcement of the Good News, is expanded into early Christian didache (the Greek word for teaching or instruction). The burden of this instruction is the triadic presence of God, who is Father, Son, and Holy Spirit. This is the doctrine (as we call it, not with entire felicity) of the functional Trinity, the Trinity-with-us. With the brevity appropriate to our present purposes, which have not to do with the complete theology of the New Testament, this doctrine may be stated in three simple propositions.

First, God still remains the one God of the Old Testament. Only now, the Name *God* has a new supposition, in the technical sense. It stands for the Father. He is now *the* God. Everywhere in St. Paul and St. John that one encounters the word God, one should read, as its sense and as the direction of its address, "the Father." This is now God's proper Name. He is "the Father of our Lord Jesus Christ" in whose manifestation as Son the Name of God was newly revealed. Second, Jesus Christ, the Son who was sent down into our midst by the

27

Father, himself bears the divine Name. He is the Lord-of-us, empowered to exercise the divine functions that the Name implies, that is, to be Savior and Judge. Third, the Father who is the one God and the Son who is the Lord-of-us are present in us through the Holy Spirit, the Spirit of the Father and of the Son, who is sent by them to be the Lord-with-us, the life-giving Lord, the indwelling Spirit of our adoption, by whom we are empowered to address God by his proper Name, "Abba, that is, Father" (Romans 8:15).

This is the New Testament answer to Moses' ancient request, which is forever the human request, to know God's Name. But now the answer is to be cast in the mysterious plural of John's text (14:23) in which Christ makes the promise that "we will come" and "we will make our abode" with the new people of God. Hence, the ancient text must now read: "We shall be there as who we are shall we be there." The Son is here with us. With him the Father, who sent him, inseparably comes to us. Here with us, Father and Son breathe into us the Holy Spirit who is their Gift, now given to us. The Three are here as who they are, mysteriously the one God, the triunely Holy One. As triune, God is more hidden than ever, more unknown, his Name more mysterious. Yet his Name has been revealed. As Father he is more intimately known, and he is more than ever truly named by all the many names that had long been used but are now laden with new meaning because they are read by men from the new works of God in our midst, more wonderful than ever—the Son's ransoming deed of love, and the Spirit's ceaseless energizing in the Church. Thus stated in triadic terms, the New Testament problematic of the presence of God exhibits a substance that transcends the Old Testament substance. At the same time, the Old Testament structure of the problem remains unchanged; the four questions return, with new meaning.

Moreover, the Old Testament alternative modes of resolution reappear. They are, still, knowledge of God or ignorance of God. The knowledge is again a recognition; what matters is to recognize the living God in "the moment of visitation" (Luke 19:42, 44) when the Word speaks, when the Spirit leads (Romans 8:13). The recognition is practical; as in the Old Testament, it takes the form of a "going with" the Spirit who is the Lord-with-us. The doctrine is developed by St. Paul, with whom the term *epignosis* becomes a technical theological term. This "knowledge (epignosis) of the truth" (1 Timothy 2:4) is both affirmation and choice, a knowledge and an acknowledgment, at once an assent and a consent, an affair of both mind and heart. It is a finding of the living God and also an endless search for him, precisely because he is the living God, present in the moment, most faithfully becoming with each fleeting moment the Lord-with-us. This Pauline epignosis is the New Testament affirmative resolution of the problem of God.

In the Bible, the problem of God is raised and answered on the level of the religious existence. Moses' question stands forever as the religious question: "Is God with us, here and now?" This is what every man born into this world and inescapably destined to a religious existence needs to know and must find out. The structure of the problem was shaped in the Old Testament. In the New Testament, within the same structure, the substance of the problem was given its definitive formulation in trinitarian terms. The formulation was as final as the promise that sustains it was faithful: "I am with you all the days, until the end of the age" (Matthew 28:20). This promise of the Son, who is the Word of God, was the echo, clearer and more resonant than the original utterance, of the word of God in Exodus, in which God spoke his Name, and thus made his promise, to Moses. Moreover, as the New Testament formulation of the problem—with its matrix in the event of Christ and with its four resultant questions—was definitive, so the resolution of the problems in terms of the Pauline epignosis is likewise definitive.

But to say this is to raise a further issue. Would it then be true to say that for the faithful Christian the problem of God has vanished? Have all the questions been answered? Are there no more questions to be asked? This is the issue with which my next chapter will deal. The answer to it is both yes and no.

THE THEOLOGICAL PROBLEM:
THE UNDERSTANDING
OF GOD

MATTHEW ARNOLD speaks somewhere of the contrast between the religious atmosphere of his own day, dusty with depressing doubt, and the New Testament climate of "boundless certitude and exhilaration." There is justice in the remark. The "bloody thread" of conflict indeed runs through New Testament history; one traces it clearly in the Acts of the Apostles. But it is evident to the reader of the "Gospel of the Holy Spirit," as this beautiful book has been called, that the men of the New Testament were not caught up in anxious questionings about God. They were absorbed in a serene quest for him, living, present through his Spirit, hidden in their midst. The problem of God as it arose out of the matrix of the event of Christ was resolved for them in terms of St. Paul's epignosis, a knowledge of God as present, an acknowledgment of his presence.

Later history, however, clearly witnesses that all the questions were not at an end; the problem of God had not been answered in all its dimensions. On the contrary, the very fact that a resolution of the problem had been found on the plane of the religious existence only served to move it into a new phase. After certain preliminary disputes, which we cannot here consider, the new problem broke out in the fourth century in one of history's most resounding and fateful controversies. It concerned the theological understanding of the New Testament revelation of the Name of God—that he is the Father who through the Son and in the Holy Spirit is the one God-with-us.

I realize that in dealing with the patristic era I shall be venturing on ground that may be unfamiliar. Recently, on consulting the catalogue of a venerable American university, noted for its academic catholicity, I found that, of one hundred and eighty-three courses offered in philosophy and religion, only three dealt explicitly with the patristic era. This is surely regrettable. It was a brilliant epoch in the history of thought, which rivalled and perhaps surpassed the fifth century B.C., when the Greek mind reached the height of its powers. The roster of the Fathers of the Church is a roll call of memorable names. And these great minds were not engaged in trivial logomachy. They carried on what was perhaps the last great religious argument of the Western world. Certainly in no subsequent argument have the issues been wrought out so clearly and argued with such amplitude for stakes that were incalculably high. In the third, fourth, and fifth centuries, the Christian mind, tutored both in faith and in philosophy, clashed in stern encounter with its two deadliest enemies, Gnostic syncretism and Hellenistic rationalism. For some of us, these still are the enemies; in new forms, they are recognizable among us today.

What were the issues? Three stand out. First, there was the issue of Christian faith in its relation both to Hebrew religion and to Greek culture. Was it possible to combine, in some harmonious synthesis, these three divergent modes of thought and styles of life, so as to create a new style of life and thought, the Christian style? Second, there was the issue of the nature of reality and of the power of intelligence to reach it. What are the ultimate categories of the real in terms of which the mind conceives and affirms that which is? Are they the categories of space, time, and matter as in Stoic materialism or the categories of ideas as in the Platonic tradition? Are they the intersubjective categories of Hebrew thought, "I and Thou," or are they the categories of being and substance as in the tradition of metaphysical realism that originated in Aristotle and was renewed and transformed by its contact with the tradition of biblical realism? Third, there was the issue of scriptural exegesis. What is the sense (or the senses) of Scripture? How does one construct a valid hermeneutic by which they may be reached? Included prominently here was the issue of symbol and reality and their relation. Specifically, what is the reality that the symbols of Scripture symbolize?

It would not be difficult, if there were time, to show that these three issues, altered in form but enduring in substance, still burn brightly today. Perhaps I should rather say that they are obscurely smoking. The issues are with us, but they are being badly argued. This, however, is another subject.

The Nicene Problem

In and through these three pervasive issues runs the fundamental problematical theme, which was the problem of God in its new form, the problem of the Logos, the Word, the Son of God, in his relation to the Father. In order to grasp the new problematic fully, one must have in mind the three component elements contained in the Christian conception of God at the time. First, there was the heritage from the Old Testament. There is one Lord, who is the living God, the Holy One hidden in the midst of the people, known through his active existence in their history. Second, there was the New Testament heritage. The same one God of the Old Testament is the Father of the Lord Jesus Christ. The Father is *the* God, God with the definite article (in Greek, *ho theos*), the one God, as Christ is the one Lord. So, in the primitive confession of faith recorded by St. Paul: "For us there is one God the Father, from whom all things [come forth], and we [go back] toward him, and one Lord Jesus Christ, through whom all things [come forth], and we [go back to the Father] through him" (1 Corinthians 8:6; the verbs of motion are only implied in the text). Third, there was the heritage common to both Old and New Testaments which is also, in some form, the patrimony of human reason itself. The one God is the Lord of the cosmic universe as its Creator, and he is likewise the Lord of history as its Ruler. This one Lord is radically distinct from the whole realm of his creation, both cosmic and historical. His power is of an order totally different from that of the forces that operate in the material universe or in the temporal process. In the customary images, he is above the world as he is outside of time. I would note here that biblical thought, like primitive thought in general, made little or no distinction between a power and the nature behind it, or between action and the power behind it. Insofar as the notion of being was conceived at all, it was conceived as constituted by power and action.

This common heritage was contained in the notion of God as Pantokrator. We translate this Greek word (taken from the Septuagint, the Alexandrian Greek translation of the Hebrew Scriptures) as "the Almighty." We hear in the word the notion of omnipotence, a power that is without limit: "God can do

34

everything." This, however, is a post-Augustinian notion. The Israelite and the early Christian heard in the word a more concrete meaning: "God the Pantokrator does everything." The reference is to an actuality of power, to the fact that the divine action, both creative and provident, is universal in its scope, extending over the whole world of nature and of man and including under its dominion all processes whatever, whether cosmic or historical.

Today, when we want to express the heritage common to the Old and New Testaments and also to the tradition of reason, we use the term *monotheism*. Its connotations are static, or, if you will, ontological. The early Christian, however, used the term *monarchy*. It is a technical theological term whose connotations are dynamic, or historical. When, for instance, Dionysius of Rome (ca. A.D. 260) speaks of the "most venerable preaching of the Church of God, which is the Monarchy," he means the traditional Hebraic and Christian doctrine of the Pantokrator—that the one Lord God is the supreme, universal, actively ruling Power over all things. It was this doctrine of the Monarchy that sustained the Christian polemic against Manichaean dualism, against the Stoic World-Soul, against the Platonic Idea of the Good, against the Gnostic Pleroma, and against all other false or faulty theologies. It was a doctrine full of mystery, inspiring awe. It was also a doctrine that presented complications, which in turn gave rise to questions. The complications were inherent in the data of Christian faith, which were chiefly three.

First, as Dionysius has just told us, the doctrine of the divine Monarchy—that there is one Pantokrator—is to be maintained as the true teaching of the Church. Second, also to be maintained as true, is the teaching that Jesus Christ is the Lord, that is, he is the Pantokrator. Third, no less to be maintained, is the truth that is evident on every page of the Gospel, that Christ, the Pantokrator, is the Son; he is from the Father and therefore is other than the Father, who is *the* God, the Pantokrator. These data of faith, which affirm a mystery, also give rise to a problem. The issue is clear. How is the ancient doctrine of the Monarchy to be maintained so as to leave intact the new doctrine that Christ, the Father's Son and Word, is equally Pantokrator, as the Father also is? This was the Nicene problem of God. It was the problem of the Logos, the Son, within the divine Monarchy. It does not rise formally on the plane of the religious existence but on the plane of theological understanding.

It is impossible to give here even a sketch of the swirling dialectic of thought that was released when Christian thinkers confronted the problem of God in its first specifically Christian form. I shall mention, however, the two major attempts at solution—by Tertullian (ca. A.D. 160—222–23) in the West, and by Origen (ca. A.D. 185–86—254–55) in the East.

Tertullian resolved the problem in the plastic terms of imagination. He cast two analogies to explain how the Son is Lord and Pantokrator simultaneously as the Monarchy remains one and undivided. Tertullian's first analogy was biological; he took it from Stoic physics, which explained the constitution of the world by analogy to the living body. The Monarchy, he said, is preserved by apprehending it as an organism. The Father and the Son are indeed parts of it, but the organism itself is undivided and its Power is one. The trouble here is that to speak of God as an organism is to use a metaphor, an analogy from the material world, to which God bears no likeness at all. Therefore, the metaphorical solution leaves the problem just as it was. The metaphor of organism serves to restate the problem in an image, but metaphors, here as everywhere else, explain nothing.

Tertullian's second analogy was anthropological. The Monarchy, he said, is preserved by apprehending Father and Son as united in a complete harmony of mind and will. The trouble here is that this is anthropomorphism, an analogy taken from the world of men. The one God, Father and Son, is utterly unlike two men who are one in spirit, united in some common enterprise. Again, the problem is left intact. Both of Tertullian's imaginative efforts fail precisely because they are imaginative. They transpose the problem to the plane of images, where no solution is available, since the problem exists in the order of thought.

In the East, Origen, the greatest genius of the third century and perhaps of any century, attacked the problem in higher terms. He made use of a concept borrowed from the most popular contemporary philosophy, Middle Platonism. It was the dyadic conception, derived from Plato himself. There is the One, the Goodness that is divine. There is also the Logos, which emanates from the One and participates in the One as the Image of the divine Goodness. The Christian doctrine of the Father and his Logos is then interpreted in terms of this Platonist scheme. The Father is *the* God; only of him does Origen use the definite article. The Logos is not *the* God; he is simply God, and he is God by emanation and participation in a Platonist sense. Therefore, he is a God "of the second order," as Origen calls him. He is a diminished deity, since emanation, in Platonist thought, involves some measure of degradation in the order of being.

This, with drastic brevity, is Origen's answer to the pre-Nicene problem of God, the Logos in the Monarchy. The trouble is that it destroys the terms of the problem. In Origen's solution, the Logos is subordinated to the Father as an inferior god who does not merit and cannot properly be given the divine Name. This is contrary to the terms of the problem as set by Christian faith, which affirms the Logos-Son to be Kyrios, Lord, the bearer of the divine Name Pantokrator in an undiminished divine sense.

Origen himself, I should add, made this Christian affirmation with complete fidelity and great vigor. But he undertook a further task, which was to set forth a theological understanding of this affirmation. His failure, like Tertullian's, was of the order of understanding. The best philosophical instrument of understanding within Origen's reach—the Middle Platonist theory of the emanation of the Logos from the One—broke in his hands. It delivered only a subordinationist theory of the Logos. This is not an understanding of the Christian doctrine of the Logos. The Christian Logos is not subordinate or inferior to the Father; to attempt to understand him thus is not to understand him at all. Origen's genial speculations had an enormous influence on subsequent theological thought, but they left the pre-Nicene problem of God standing, still awaiting the construction of a theology that would be adequate to the problem.

As a matter of fact, the issue of the alternatives, which is essential to the notion of a problem, had not yet been stated with precision. This was finally done by Arius, a priest of Alexandria and director of the school of exegesis there, an able dialectician, a disciple of Lucian of Antioch, trained in Lucian's famous school. His greatest historical significance was that he ruthlessly clarified the problem of the Logos and set it in its proper terms.

The new clarity is evident to anyone who reads Arius' profession of his personal faith, written about 318 in a letter to Alexander, the bishop of Alexandria, which has been preserved for us by Athanasius. Arius impatiently discards all metaphor and all anthropomorphism; he dismisses all Platonist speculation. Instead, he posits the question in categories completely alien to all the philosophical and religious systems of the ancient world. He asks his question in the Hebraic-Christian categories of Creator and creature. Arius' question was luminously clear. Given that the Son is from the Father, is the Son of the order of the Creator, who is God, or of the order of the creature, who is not God? And to the question thus put, in altogether decisive form, he returns an unequivocal answer. The Son, he says, is from the Father as the "perfect creature." He came to be as all creatures come to be, through a making, through an act of the Father's will. When he thus became, he came to be out of nothing. And before he came to be, he was not. Therefore "there was when he was not" (this last phrase is the celebrated Arian tessera that shocked the Christian world).

This was Arius' answer to the problem of the Logos within the Monarchy. He rescues the Monarchy by extruding the Logos from it. It was the answer of the rationalist who eliminates the seeming contradictions within the Christian statement of the mystery of God by evacuating the mystery itself. In the end, for Arius, the Logos-Son has only the status of a creature; he is no more a mystery than you or I.

We need not be concerned here with the case Arius made for his view. It was essentially a dialectical, not a scriptural, case. It was based on the notion of God as the Unoriginate and on the conclusion that what originates from God, as the Son from the Father, must necessarily be created. It is more to our purpose here to note the mode of thought in which Arius raised the problem of the Son. His question asked whether the Son *is* God or not. The correlative questions were, what does it mean to say that the Son *is-from* the Father as Son, that is, what *is* his mode of origin from the Father and what therefore *is* his relation to the Father? I add emphasis to illustrate the fact that these were ontological questions. They raised the issue of the being and substance of the Son as he *is,* in himself and in relation to the Father. Moreover, the alternative answers which Arius presented and from which he chose were cast in ontological categories, God or creature. These are categories of being and substance. They transcend the Stoic materialist categories, the idealist categories of Platonist devising, and the intersubjective categories of Hebraic thought.

Four comments need to be made on Arius' position of the problem of the Son. It was new, inevitable, legitimate, and exigent of an answer that would have to be an answer of faith.

In the first place, the Arian question was new in the form and mode of thought in which Arius raised it. The New Testament problem had been that of the presence of the Son, and with him the Father, in the midst of the people as Savior and Judge. Explicitly, therefore, the problem had been stated in the intersubjective category of presence with its attendant dynamic categories of power, function, and action. The Christology of the New Testament was, in our contemporary word for it, functional. For instance, all the titles given to Christ the Son—Lord, Savior, Word, Son of God, Son of man, Messiah, Prophet, Priest—all these titles, in the sense that they bear in the New Testament, are relational. They describe what Christ is to us; they detail his functions in regard to our salvation. They do not explicitly define what he *is,* nor do they explicitly define what his relation to the Father is. Therefore, in asking whether the Son *is* God or not, Arius altered the scriptural state of the question. He moved the problem into a different universe of discourse. In effect, he asked a new question.

In the second place, it was inevitable that the new question should have been asked. If Arius had not asked it, someone else would have. There are two reasons for its inevitability.

The first lies in the essential dynamism of human intelligence. When it functions without any bias induced by faulty or prejudicial training, the mind moves inevitably from the question of what things are to us (the phenomenological question) to the deeper question of what things are in themselves (the ontological question). The human mind moves from description to definition. In this case, it moves from inquiry into the reality of God's presence to inquiry into the reality of the God who is present. The biblical question, whether God is with us, is organically related to the patristic question, what the God-who-is-with-us *is*.

The second reason for the inevitability of Arius' question lies in the realist conception of the word of God contained in Scripture and unanimously held in the Church of the Fathers. At that time, there was no doubt in anyone's mind that the Scriptures were not simply the record of the religious experience of Isaiah or Ezechiel, of Paul or John. In the patristic era, the Christian did not consider that his faith was based on religious experience, his own or that of anyone else. It was based on the events of the sacred history—the event of Christ supervening on the ancient events of the history of Israel. He knew that in these events, which were irruptions of the divine into history, God was the "speaking God" of the Letter to the Hebrews (1:1). He knew that the word spoken by God came from Intelligence and was addressed to an intelligence. It was suffused with mystery, but it was nonetheless compact of conceptions that were somehow intelligible and of affirmations that were unconditionally true. He knew, finally, that, since they were true (as warranted by the "speaking God"), the affirmations in the word of God put him in touch with reality. They had for him an ontological reference. They were not mere symbols whose value would be as vehicles of man's religious experience, which would itself then be the ultimately real. The value of the word of God was in its truth, in the fact that it affirmed what is, what exists in an order related indeed to man's religious experience but only because it is itself antecedently real. So, when the Christian cried, "Lord Jesus!", he was not simply uttering his religious experience of the risen Jesus. He was affirming that Jesus did rise from the dead and that he is the Lord.

It was this conviction of the realism of the word of God—that it is a real word with a real meaning—that sustained Athanasius in working out the celebrated formula which explained the sense inherent in the dogma stated by the Council of Nicaea. His study of the Scriptures disclosed to him, as to Basil later, a general proposition. All the affirmations made by the Scriptures about the Father are also made about the Son, with one exception. The Scriptures never say that the Son is the Father. In particular, the Scriptures affirm about the Son what they affirm about the Father, that he has as his own the two powers that are uniquely divine and proper only to God—the power to give life and the power to judge the heart of man. If, then, everything that is true about the Father is likewise true about the Son, except that the Son is not the Father, it follows that the Son *is* all that the Father *is*, except for the Name of Father.

This was the Athanasian rule of faith, based on the Scriptures, which the Council of Nicaea had stated in a dogmatic formula, as we shall see. The point at the moment is that behind the Athanasian rule lay the universal patristic conviction that, to put the matter in our technical terms, a realist epistemology and ontology are implicit in the conception of the word of God which the Scriptures exhibit. The word of God is true; therefore it expresses what is.

In the third place, it follows that the Arian form of the pre-Nicene question, whether the Son is God or a creature, was entirely legitimate. The reason is that it was stated in ontological categories that were undeniably scriptural. If the Old and New Testaments affirm anything at all, they affirm that the Creator *is* God and that the creature *is* a creature. These affirmations are not a matter of religious experience but of ontology. These two categories, Creator and creature, are classifications of being. They define things that are and that are radically distinct in the order of substance. It was therefore legitimate to state the problem of the Logos in these ontological terms.

In the fourth and final place, because the Arian ontological question was new and had not been explicitly answered, because it was inevitable and had to arise, because it was legitimate and could not be declined, it demanded an answer. More than that, the answer had to be the answer of faith. The Arian question had not been raised in the spirit of detached Hellenistic speculation, as an interesting problem for leisurely and inconclusive discussion in the school. On the contrary, upon the answer to the question hung the whole issue of human salvation.

All through the Arian controversy runs the soteriological argument for the full divinity of the Son. Its premise was the doctrine, as old as the Old Testament itself, that only God can save us. Only he is the Power that can rescue us from death in all the forms that death takes and bring us to life in the land of integrity and peace that he has promised to the faithful. Hence, from Athanasius onward, the Fathers argue that, if the Son is not God, fully the Pantokrator, wholly situated within the order of the divine power and being, then he is not our Savior and we are not saved. It was clear to the Fathers that there was no salvation in the Arian Son, a time-bound creature such as we are, out of the Father by a making as we are, Son only by a grace that holds no grace for us.

The imperious Arian question received its definitive answer at the Council of Nicaea in 325, at the hands of the Fathers assembled in the legendary number of three hundred and eighteen. Their complicated preliminary debates need not detain us. In the end they composed the creed that is familiar to the whole Christian world. "We believe," they wrote, "in one God the Father, the Pantokrator, Maker of all things visible and invisible; and in one Lord Jesus Christ, the Son of God, begotten out of the Father, the Only-begotten." So far one hears only the echo of earlier creeds, themselves the echo of the scriptural formulas. Then comes the cutting edge of the Nicene dogma that thrust through all the Arian evasions to the essential issue: "Begotten out of the Father, that is, out of the substance of the Father, God out of God, Light out of Light, true God out of true God." The Son is not out of the Father's will, as the creature is, but out of his substance, by a unique mode of origination radically different from the creative act. The Christian alternative in the Arian dichotomy, God or creature, is selected and posited: "Begotten, not made." The Son is not the perfect creature, placed, by a making, outside of the divine order. He is begotten within the divine order and he remains within it. His being is untouched by createdness. Finally, there comes the famous word to which a century of argument had inevitably moved: "Consubstantial (*homoousion*) with the Father."

In the adjective *homoousion* the Nicene problem of God finds its definitive answer. The answer is given, as it had to be given, not in the empirical categories of experience, the relational category of presence, or, even, the dynamic categories of power and function but in the ontological category of substance, which is a category of being. Nicaea did not describe; it defined. It defined what the Son is, in himself and in his relation to the one God the Father. The Son is from the Father in a singular, unshared way, begotten as Son, not made as a creature. The Son is all that the Father is, except for the Name of Father. This is what homoousion means. This is what the Son is.

Two aspects of the Nicene dogma call for comment. It was not new, and it was new.

It was not a new truth, not a new revelation. The intention of the Nicene Fathers was simply to state the sense of the Scriptures against the Arian dialectical distortion. Athanasius is explicitly clear on this point. The difficulty was that the sense of the Scriptures with regard to what the Son is was scattered in a multiplicity of affirmations about him. It was contained in all the titles given him, in all the symbols and images used of him, in all the predicates that describe his role and function concerning our salvation. All that Nicaea did was to reduce the multiplicity of the scriptural affirmations to the unity of a single affirmation. The Son, begotten from the Father, not made by him, is consubstantial with the Father— this was the sense of everything that the Scriptures had to say about the Son. Therefore it was nothing new. It had already been said.

The Nicene dogma was new, however, in that it stated the sense of the Scriptures in a new mode of understanding that was not formally scriptural. The Scriptures had affirmed that Jesus Christ, the Son, is here with us as Lord of us. Nicaea affirmed that the Lord Jesus Christ is the consubstantial Son. The sense of both affirmations is the same, but the mode of conception and statement is different. A passage has been made from a conception of what Christ the Son is-to-us to a conception of what the Son, Christ, is-in-himself. The transition is from a mode of understanding that is descriptive, relational, interpersonal, historical-existential, to a mode of understanding that is definitive, explanatory, absolute, ontological. The alteration in the mode of understanding does not change the sense of the affirmation, but it does make the Nicene affirmation new in its form.

At the Council itself the reason for the passage to the new ontological mode of conception and statement was altogether practical. Athanasius is again explicit on this point. The old efforts to state the doctrine of the Son and Logos used scriptural formulas; this had been the traditional practice, visible in all the earlier creeds. The trouble was that the Arian party was quite willing to recite the scriptural affirmations at the same time that it read into them an Arian understanding, the conception of the Son as a creature. The Fathers had, therefore, to go beyond the letter of the scriptural formulas to their sense. They stated the sense in new formulas, "out of the substance of the Father," "consubstantial with the Father." These formulas would not bear the Arian understanding. The latter was excluded from the formulas by the new mode of understanding the Scriptures that the formulas embodied.

The new formulas were not adopted without opposition, either at the Council or in the course of the long controversy that ensued. They were opposed, of course, by the men of the radical Arian Left and by their leftist successors, the so-called Half-Arians. But they were also opposed by the men of the conservative Right, the "men around Eusebius of Caesarea," and later by the party led by Acacius, the successor to Eusebius in the see of Caesarea. The essential refusal of the Right can be seen, for instance, in the so-called "Dated Creed," which was the formula published by the Fourth Synod of Sirmium in 359. This document forbids all mention of *ousia* (substance) when there is question of the Catholic faith, on the ground that "nowhere in the Scriptures is there mention of *ousia* in regard of Father and Son." The conservative position is stated thus: "We say that the Son is like (*homoios*) in all things to the Father, just as the Scriptures say and teach." The same essential conservative position is visible in the formula of the Synod of Constantinople in 361. The homoousion, it said, is not a scriptural word; therefore the Nicene formula cannot be a formula of faith.

The prime objection of the Right was to the word, but the issue went much deeper, below the level of language, to an issue of most weighty substance. The real issue concerned development in the understanding of the Christian revelation and faith. It concerned progress within the tradition. This was the issue that the Eusebians, after the immemorial custom of conservatives, failed to see or, perhaps, refused to see. They pretended to be the protagonists of the tradition. In fact, they were only defenders of the status quo, which is quite a different thing. They were fundamentalists, or biblical positivists. They were in their own way the first proponents of the maxim, "Sola Scriptura," in their insistence that only in the formulas of Scripture may the Christian faith be proposed.

Some of them, like Eusebius of Caesarea, were scholars, but

he, for all his historical learning, was a muddle-headed old man, as he has been rightly called. His head was muddled largely by his politics. He was, as the fifth-century Church historian Socrates called him, "two-faced," one face looking to the Emperor, the other to the Church. The majority of the Right were not scholars but practical men, like Acacius. He was trying to run a diocese in a troubled time within the Empire, and he chiefly wanted peace. Let us agree, he said in effect, to say what the Scriptures say and have done with it. Since he was only a practical man, with no great theological or exegetical mind, it did not occur to him that what he and his followers were saying at the Synod of Constantinople—that the Son is "like in all things to the Father"—was not, in point of fact, what the Scriptures said. As the orthodox Center rightly insisted, the Scriptures say that the Son is consubstantial with the Father. This is identically the sense of the scriptural affirmation, though the Scriptures state it only in the distinctively scriptural mode of understanding. It was the Center, Athanasius and his party, that stood for the tradition by standing for progress within the tradition, for an orderly growth of the tradition, for a higher and more exact understanding of what the tradition affirms. The Right, in contrast, was reactionary, or, to put it more elegantly, they were victims of the fallacy of archaism.

At the root of the fallacy is the rejection of the notion that Christian understanding of the affirmations of faith can and indeed must grow, at the same time that the sense of the affirmations remains unaltered. Archaist Eusebian thought wanted to cling to the earlier stage of understanding contained in the letter of Scripture, as later archaist thought would want to return to it—return from the complexities of conciliar dogma to the "simple faith of the fishermen of Galilee." The trouble is that one cannot thus put back the clock of thought.

The Eusebians were trying to meet today's question with yesterday's answer, but the question of the day was new. Arius had cast the old question in a new mode of conception, the ontological mode. It was no longer to be answered simply by repeating the formulas of Scripture, which did not directly meet the new issue because their affirmations were made in a different mode of understanding. Nor would it suffice to evade the Arian issue by recourse to ambiguous formulas like the *homoios,* the notion that the Son is "like" the Father.

What the Eusebians further failed to see was that the fallacy of archaism inevitably breeds its contrary, which is the fallacy of futurism. The futurist fallacy rests on the notion that the affirmations of Christian faith never have a final sense. They are constantly subject to reinterpretation in terms of any sort of contemporary philosophical thought. Development in the understanding of them is altogether open-ended. It may move in any direction, even to the dissolution of the original sense of the Christian affirmations. It was the merit of the Athanasian Center that it saw how dangerous the archaism of the Eusebians was. The Athanasians perceived that it opened the way to the futurism of Arius, who reinterpreted the scriptural affirmations—that the Father is Unoriginate and that the Son originates from the Father—in terms of a rationalist dialectic to the destruction of the sense of the scriptural faith.

The Nicene homoousion avoids both fallacies, archaism and futurism. It transposes the scriptural affirmations concerning the Son into a new mode of understanding—what we now call the Nicene or dogmatic mode for the reason that the Nicene dogma was its first historical illustration. But there is no discontinuity or incoherence between the dogmatic mode and the scriptural mode. The transition from one to the other was not made violently—from the descriptive, relational, interpersonal, historical-existential, scriptural mode, to the definitive, absolute, explanatory, ontological, dogmatic mode. The passage was made with ease and naturalness on the internal authority that it is in accord with the native dynamism of intelligence. Between the two modes there is harmony, even homogeneity. The sense of the affirmation, as made in both modes, is identical. The sense of Scripture, that Jesus, the Son, is present as our Lord, is identically the sense of Nicaea, that Jesus, our Lord, is consubstantially the Son. The tradition is maintained. But there has been progress within it, growth in the understanding of it. The homoousion formulates the traditional faith; it is a formula of faith. But the faith is so formulated as now to be more fully understood. The Christian who affirmed that Christ is with us as the Lord still makes this affirmation, only now he has come to understand more fully what Christ, the Lord with us, *is*. He has transcended archaism, and, in so doing, he has also avoided futurism.

The homoousion represents a limit in the understanding of the faith. As there is no stopping short of it on peril of archaist imprecision in the faith, so there is no going beyond it on peril of futurist adulteration of the faith. The homoousion is a limit in another sense. The three data of faith that it synthesizes are data of mystery—that the one God the Father is Pantokrator, that the Lord Jesus Christ, the Son, is Pantokrator, and that the Son is from the Father and other than Father. The homoousion resolves the seeming contradiction. If, as the homoousion asserts, the Son is all that the Father is, except for the Name of Father, then the Son is Pantokrator as the Father is, but he is not the Father. But here intelligence has reached its limit. The problem is solved, to the limits of solution. The mystery remains intact, adorable.

We cannot here follow the complicated convolutions of

the post-Nicene argument that ran to its close in the Council of Constantinople in 381. Then the doctrine of the homoousion was applied to the Holy Spirit, at least in its substance, though in a different verbal form. We believe, so runs the third major article in the Nicene-Constantinopolitan creed, "in the Holy Spirit, who is the Lord and the Giver of life, who proceeds from the Father, who with the Father and the Son is to be equally worshipped and honored." The definition was the answer to the special problem of the Holy Spirit that had been raised in the final phase of the Arian controversy. This problem is a subject in itself, not to be touched here. There is, however, a reason for stating the wider and more far-reaching significance of the Nicene definition for later Christian history. Five aspects of it should be noted.

First, as I have pointed out, the Nicene definition was a rejection of Eusebian archaism and its effort to restrict the Christian faith to the formulas of Scripture. Second, the definition formally established the statute of the ontological mentality within the Church. It was the precedent for the Councils of Ephesus and Chalcedon, which resolved the issue of the internal constitution of Christ, the Son Incarnate, in the ontological categories of nature and person. In doing this the two Councils forbade the freezing of the Christian faith in patristic formulas. This had been the basic issue in the confused Christological controversies that preceded Chalcedon. It was again an issue of archaism. Third, by its passage from the historical-existential categories of Scripture to the ontological or explanatory categories exhibited in the homoousion, Nicaea sanctioned the principle of the development of doctrine—the phrase is Newman's. It is not a sufficiently revealing phrase. One might better speak of growth in understanding of the primitive affirmations contained in the New Testament revelation. What emerges in the course of this growth is not some totally new affirmation but a new understanding of an affirmation already made in another mode of conception or, perhaps, only obscurely, implicitly, confusedly, as a virtuality. Fourth, by thus sanctioning the principle of doctrinal growth, Nicaea established a bridge between Scripture and conciliar dogma, joining these distinct territories into the one country that is the Catholic unity of faith. Scripture states the faith of the Church; so does dogma, but in another mode of conception and statement so organically related to the scriptural didache as to merit the name of growth. Fifth and finally, by sanctioning the status of the ontological mentality in the field of faith, Nicaea also established the statute of the philosophical reason in the field of theology. Thus, it laid down the charter of Scholasticism. Without Nicaea there would have been no Chalcedon; in a different way, without Nicaea there would have been no Thomas Aquinas. Indeed, there would have been no Augustine.

The reason I record these five aspects of the import of the Nicene homoousion is that they lead to insight into the basic issues that are today crucial in the ecumenical dialogue. The relation between Scripture and dogma, between Holy Writ and Holy Church, or, more generally, between sacred history and sacred doctrine—surely this is a basic issue in the ecumenical argument. Basic, too, is the relation between Christian faith and philosophical theology—more generally, the relation between faith and reason or, in a narrower sense, the relation between the methodological technique proper to secular historiography and the technique proper to the investigation of the unique type of history found in the Old and New Testaments. But the most basic and pervasive issue is the one recognized by Newman: the development of doctrine. Leaving aside the issue of what Catholic and Protestant respectively mean when they say, "Credo," I consider that the parting of the ways between the two Christian communities takes place on the issue of development of doctrine.

That development has taken place in both communities cannot possibly be denied. The question is, what is legitimate development, what is organic growth in the understanding of the original deposit of faith, what is warranted extension of the primitive discipline of the Church, and what, on the other hand, is accretion, additive increment, adulteration of the deposit, distortion of true Christian discipline? The question is, what are the valid dynamisms of development and what are the forces of distortion? The question is, what are the criteria by which to judge between healthy and morbid development, between true growth and rank excrescence? The question is, what is archaism and what is futurism? Perhaps, above all, the question is, what are the limits of development and growth—the limits that must be reached on peril of archaistic stuntedness, and the limits that must not be transgressed on peril of futuristic decadence?

I am not at all sure that this whole complex issue has yet been recognized as decisive in its import for the ecumenical dialogue. I shall, however, register my own conviction in this regard. I do not think that the first ecumenical question is, what think ye of the Church? Or even, what think ye of Christ? The dialogue would rise out of the current confusion if the first question raised were, what think ye of the Nicene homoousion?

I should like briefly to discuss this question, without attempting to deal with all the ecumenical issues, listed above, that it raises.

Toward the end of the nineteenth century, a learned assault on the religious significance of the Nicene dogma was led by Adolf von Harnack (1851–1930), the coryphaeus of rationalist liberalism. He broached and elaborated, with great historical erudition, the thesis of the "Hellenization of the faith" in the patristic era. The Nicene dogma and the other conciliar dogmas that succeeded it represented, he said, the "work of the Hellenic spirit on the soil of the Gospel." The work was one of corruption. The substance of the Gospel perished under the accretions of Hellenistic ontology. The essence of Christianity was lost.

No one today holds Harnack's thesis in the form in which he presented it; it has become untenable in the light of the findings of more advanced scholarship. Biblical studies have destroyed its premise, that the essence of Christianity (*Das Wesen des Christentums,* the title of one of Harnack's famous books) consisted in little more than an inner religious sense of the Fatherhood of God. Patristic studies have disallowed Harnack's essential conclusions with regard to what really happened in the early Christian centuries. Nevertheless, Harnack's main thesis persists, in diluted form. It happens continually that theories, once seemingly supported by scholarship, survive in the popular mind long after their learned support has been undermined. One hears the Harnack thesis faintly echoed in the view that the Church of the early centuries reinterpreted the Christian faith in terms of contemporary philosophies.

This, of course, is exactly the thing that the Church did not do. This is, in fact, the thing that Nicaea (to stay with my own subject) anathematized Arius for doing. The issue here is one of historical scholarship. If one is looking for Hellenizers of the Christian faith in the pre- and post-Nicene period, one can indeed find them. In Tertullian one can find Hellenistic ontology on the Stoic model, as in Origen one can find it on the Platonist model. But both forms of Hellenism were rejected in the Nicene homoousion, which is neither a Stoic nor a

Platonist conception. Above all, one can find the Hellenic spirit in the Arian school—the rationalist spirit that would dissolve the Christian mystery of the Son by a process of corrosive dialect, destroying the essence of Christianity, which is the belief that salvation is through the Son, sent by the Father as the Lord-of-us. The Arian Son, the perfect creature, was indeed the construction of the Hellenic spirit working on the soil of the Gospel. But this Hellenic spirit and its creation were condemned in the Nicene homoousion, which re-announced, in the face of Hellenic rationalism, the mystery of Father and Son, the one Pantokrator.

The only place where one cannot find Hellenism is in the homoousion. It would be impossible to find a conception more remote from, at odds with, all the ontologies of the Graeco-Roman world than the conception embodied in this word, which says that the Son is all that the Father is except for the name of Father. In respect of its Christian meaning, the homoousion was a new coinage, a sort of Melchisedech among words, without father, without mother, without genealogy—whether Gnostic, Platonist, or Stoic. It was a technical, dogmatic coinage, struck for the purpose of declaring the sense of the Scriptures with regard to what the Son is and whence he is. It may be said that in the homoousion the Fathers of Nicaea christianized Hellenism in the single sense that they sanctioned the ontological mode of conception characteristic of the Hellenic mentality. But it may not be said, on peril of learned absurdity, that they hellenized Christianity.

If, then, in answer to the question, what think ye of the homoousion, you want to reply that it is not a valid formula of Christian faith, you will have to find other grounds than the outworn Harnackian thesis that the homoousion is Hellenism. What other grounds are there?

You may choose to reply to the ecumenical question—I say "you" in order to sustain the dramatic form of dialogue— with the assertion that the homoousion is not derivative from or a category of religious experience. Therefore, as a word and as a conception, it must be disallowed in Christian use. But this is to raise a prior issue. The issue is, whether the categories of religious experience, whatever they may be, are the final and definitive categories for the utterance of the Christian faith.

More fundamentally, this reply would raise the issue of the word of God—what is it? Is it to be identified with its effect in experience in such wise that what I experience is what God said? In other words, on hearing the word of God, am I, in effect, simply talking to myself or is the word of God really a word, the utterance of Another, a thing of meaning, which contains conceptions and affirmations that were embodied in it by the Speaker and not by me? The homoousion represents a position taken on this issue. Its premise is a realist doctrine of the word of God, the conviction that a realist epistemology and ontology are inherent in the biblical conception of the word of God. The homoousion is indeed the word of the Church, but it was put forward as a word of faith because it undertook to declare the sense of the word of God that God spoke in order to tell us what the Son *is*.

You may then wish, with the tradition, to attach a realist meaning to the word of God, to hold that it has an inherent sense, to maintain that it tells me what the Son *is*. If, granting this, you still wish to ban the homoousion from the vocabulary of faith, you have a choice of alternatives.

On the one hand, you can maintain that the Nicene word and the conception contained in it do not declare the sense of the scriptural word of God. This, however, is dubious ground to take. You have against you all the Fathers and Doctors of the Church, from Athanasius to John Damascene in the East and from Jerome to Isidore in the West. You are, in effect, raising the issue of tradition in its relation to the revealed and inspired scriptural word of God. The issue is whether tradition has the function of declaring the sense of the word of God so that it is itself a binding norm of faith. If so, the case for the homoousion is conclusive. If not, the ecumenical dialogue is, I presume, at an end.

If tradition does not have this function and force, it has none; that is to say, there is no tradition. Consequently, there can be no theological argument. You cannot argue any issue of theology, much less of faith, if you so jettison tradition. If the appeal to tradition as the authorized interpreter of the word of God is not valid, the whole argument descends to another level, that of sheer technical scholarship. The exegete or the historian or the archeologist will determine what the word of God says and means. But this is, on any showing, the hellenization of the Christian faith.

On the other hand, you may choose simply to maintain that the homoousion is not a scriptural word and therefore cannot be a formula of faith, whatever conception it may or may not embody. But this would be to summon from the vast deep the spirit of Eusebius of Caesarea. If he were to come, he would not call you muddle-headed. Apart from perhaps being personally sensitive on the point, he would understand that an ecumenical dialogue is in progress to which such characterizations are alien. But he would, I presume, now be in a position to point out that you are raising the issue of archaism or, more broadly, the issue of development of doctrine, of growth in Christian understanding of the word of God.

You might be willing to grant this, but then go on to say

that the development represented by the homoousion was merely the product of historical necessity. The schools in Antioch and in Alexandria, in Carthage and in Rome, had begun to talk about the Logos in terms of *ousia,* substance; therefore the Church had to fall in with this quaint custom of the historical present. But this development had a merely contingent character so that its term, the new word of the Church, remained extrinsic and heterogeneous to the word of God. But then you are raising the issue of the relation between the scriptural categories of presence and function and the dogmatic categories of being and substance. Is this relation contingent and extrinsic or is it intrinsic and essential? The concept "to be-with" is not yet, indeed, formally the concept "to be," but the question is whether both concepts do not contain, in different ways, a reference to what *is*—an ontological reference that must somehow terminate at substantial being either as it is present or as it is in itself. If you wish to speak, as the word of God does, about the reality of the presence of Christ, the Son and Lord, to his new people, you can hardly avoid saying something, as the Church did, about the reality of the Son and Lord who is present.

In other words, you are raising the issue of the relation between the two basic modes of human thought, the descriptive and the explanatory. The issue is whether the passage from description of a thing-in-its-function-in-regard-to-me to definition of the thing-in-its-subsistence-as-a-thing-in-itself is sheerly contingent and historical or necessary and essential. More simply, the issue is whether the definition of a thing is inherent in or extrinsic to the description of it. Concretely, was the word of the Church (which defined what the Son is-in-himself) an accretion and an addition to the word of God (which described what the Son is-to-us) to the effect that the definition and the description remain heterogeneous and therefore cannot both be words of faith, or was the explanatory word of the Church simply an organic growth in understanding of the descriptive word of God to the effect that the two words are homogeneous and therefore both words of faith, intrinsically related as two ways of understanding the same one faith, whose one object is the Son and Lord?

The matter grows complicated. You may therefore wish to transcend, and thus avoid, the whole issue by saying that the faith of the Christian cannot be made subject to the test of a formula against which its orthodoxy is to be judged. This is again to raise the issue of tradition. Certainly the Nicene Fathers and the faithful of their churches, and after them the faithful of the universal Church, considered that such a test was legitimate, valid, and necessary. The creed that they composed was not a baptismal creed, a simple profession of faith, a mosaic of scriptural phrases. It was a "bishop's creed," as it has been aptly called. It was deliberately designed as a test of orthodoxy. This is why it went beyond the traditional formulas of Scripture, in order to make sure that the affirmations in the tradition would be understood by all the bishops and by all the faithful in the same single sense, in the only sense in which the word of God may be rightly understood. You may say that the Nicene Fathers were in error in thus subjecting the faith of Christians to the test of a formula. *Securus iudicat orbis terrarum.* It may be, however, that they were not in error, in which case the error would be to say that they were in error.

The foregoing is altogether a skeletal form of the ecumenical argument. It may even be that the skeleton is missing an arm or a leg or a few bones from the breast cage. I merely wanted to illustrate what I take to be the fact, that a basic place in the dialogue may be claimed for the Nicene question, what think ye of the homoousion—is it the Christian faith or is it only philosophy?

The Eunomian Problem

There was another dimension to the problem of God in the patristic era. Arius had raised only the first pair of questions in the total problematic, the existential and the functional questions. In raising them he also transposed them into a new mode of thought. He asked a formal question of existence, whether the Lord Jesus Christ *is* the Son. He thus asked the inseparable formal question of essence, what the Son is— or more exactly, why is the Son really Son, scilicet, how is he out of the Father and what is he therefore to the Father?

There remained, however, the second pair of inseparable questions, noetic and onomastic. They had indeed been answered in the Scriptures, but the answer itself inevitably and legitimately gave rise to a new form of the paired questions. The new question concerned the theological understanding of the scriptural answer.

The answer was contained in two series of texts. One asserts that God is unknown, hidden from men, "dwelling in a light unapproachable, whom no man has seen or can see" (1 Timothy 6:16). As no man has seen his face, so no man knows his Name. The other series asserts that God is known, "not far from anyone of us" (Acts 17:27). His invisibilities, in St. Paul's phrase, are visible in the world of nature (Romans 1:20). Furthermore, he is known as Lord and Savior through the mighty deeds he did and the many words he spoke in history (Hebrews 1:2). In particular, his only-begotten Son, made man, has "brought news" of him (John 1:18). Man therefore knows God and does not know him. Man has no Name for

God, and he has many names for God. His condition is at once knowledge and non-knowledge (*gnosis* and *agnosia* are the Greek words whose assonance cannot be reproduced in English). But what can this mean and how is it to be understood? Is it contradiction or only paradox? In what sense is the Christian to be both gnostic and agnostic? The Scripture does not answer. It is not the kind of question that even arises in the historical-existential scriptural mode of thought. It is, however, a legitimate human question and therefore it inevitably had to come up for answer.

The man who raised it was Eunomius (d. 394), the leader of the radical Arian Left in the third and final phase of the Arian controversy. He was a disciple of Aetius of Antioch, a dialectician and a sophist like his master, and sometime bishop of Cyzicus until, as the historian Socrates tells us, "the people, unable to endure any longer his empty and arrogant parade of language, drove him out of their city."

Eunomius' answer to the noetic and onomastic questions was simple: "I know God," he said, "as God knows himself." On the face of it the statement seems silly. One must understand, however, that Eunomius was a nominalist. For him, as for his numerous posterity, knowledge has to do only with the names of things: a name either designates the essence of a thing or it is merely an empty sound. Eunomius said, I know the Name of God; it is Agennetos. (The Greek word can mean either "ungenerated" or, more broadly, "without origin." Newman translated it, "the Unoriginate.") As God knows his own Name, said Eunomius, so do I. And this, he added, is God's only Name. All the other many names scattered throughout the Scriptures are either empty verbalisms that say nothing about God or they are mere synonyms for Agennetos, the one divine Name.

The issue drawn by this facile dialectician was not academic.

His gnosticism and his agnosticism, both of them misplaced, made wreckage of Christianity. On the one hand, if God is known as he knows himself, he is not transcendent to human intelligence. He does not dwell in the inaccessible light of mystery. That is to say, he is not God. "If you have comprehended," St. Augustine would later say, "what you have comprehended is not God." On the other hand, if God is not really known by the many names given him from his transparency through the sacred history and through the sacral cosmos, he cannot be known at all. Therefore he is not present with us and he is not our God.

The adversaries of Eunomius were Basil of Caesarea, Gregory of Nazianzus, Basil's brother Gregory of Nyssa, and John Chrysostom. In the patristic manner, they undertook first to witness to the faith affirmed in the Scriptures. They dwelt on the primary scriptural theme that God is, in the classic technical Greek term, *Akataleptos,* the Incomprehensible. They forbade the Eunomian type of "busy scrutiny," as they called it, of the divine mystery, and they recalled to the faithful their creaturely condition, which is that of ignorance (agnosia) of God. Second, the Cappadocians (as Basil and the two Gregories are customarily called) elaborated the subordinate scriptural theme that God is both knowable and known, as he shines through the web of history and the fabric of the world. They reminded the faithful of their creaturely privilege, which is to have a knowledge (gnosis) of God and thus to have God present as the God-with-us.

To develop these two themes, however, was simply to echo the doctrine of the Scriptures. There was the further task of setting the two themes in harmony.

How and why is it that God is at once known and unknown? This question was put not to Christian faith itself, which simply affirms the fact, but to the theological intelligence, to reason illuminated by faith. The answer was found by the skills of reason, chiefly by its high art of making distinctions. Aristotle had long since distinguished the two questions that direct all intellectual inquiry because they also designate the two acts of the mind. There is the question whether a thing is (the Latin *an est,* the Greek *oti estin*), which is answered by the act of affirmation or judgment. There is the concomitant question, what the thing is (the Latin *quid est,* the Greek *ti estin*), which is answered by the act of conception or understanding. With Basil this distinction first appears in the service of the Christian faith against the destructively misplaced agnosticism and gnosticism of Eunomius. We can answer the question of existence; we can affirm, make the true judgment, that God is. But we cannot answer the question of essence; we cannot understand, grasp in a proper concept, what God is. In the order of understanding, however, a negative knowledge is available. Precisely because we affirm that God is God, we can know that he is not his creation.

In terms of this distinction, man's gnosis and his agnosia were rightly located. To the newly raised noetic question, how God is known, the patristic answer was given, that he is known in his existence but not known in his essence. I can affirm that God is and that he is all that Scriptures, or reason, say he is— eternal, omnipotent, wise, good, and so on. But I cannot conceive what it is for God to be and to be eternal, omnipotent, wise, good, and all the rest of what he is.

There was then the further inevitable onomastic question, the issue of the many names of God that designate what we call his attributes. Does each name singly, and do all of them together, express some sort of true conception or understanding of God, or are they simply the projection onto God of man's

63

understanding of himself and of his world in such wise that, when man undertakes to articulate his complex conception of God, he is merely fashioning an idol with the techniques of human intelligence? The problem is clear. The many names of God are taken from the order of human experience. How, then, can they be names of God, who does not belong to this terrestrial order?

The Fathers found a clue to the answer in the source through which they were continually searching. The Scriptures say that God is totally unlike his creation and absolutely outside of it because he is the Holy One. "I am God, not man" (Hosea 11:9). But the Scriptures also say that the creation is somehow like God and he is not wholly outside of it because it is the work of his hands and his glory dwells in it. By the glory of God the Scriptures regularly mean God himself as he is present in the world and with his people, manifesting his power, and to that extent himself, in his mighty acts, creative and redemptive.

This was a small clue indeed, but it was enough to put the Fathers on the track of the doctrine that was later known as the analogy of being. It also put them on the track of the intellectual technique that was later called the three ways of knowing God. They did not systematically elaborate the doctrine or exploit the technique. They did, however, clearly distinguish the two radically different modes of being, uncreated and created, finite and infinite, each of them real and both of them therefore somehow united in the notion of being. And they laid down the essential structure of the three ways, the dialectic movement of intelligence from the created to the uncreated order of being. There is the moment of affirmation or position. I affirm that God is or that he is good (and so on for all his attributes). There is the moment of negation or removal. I deny that God is or that he is good in the mode of being or of being good that is proper to the created order whence my notion of being and of being good was derived. There is also, supporting and pervading the dialectic of affirmation and negation, the sense of the divine transcendence. I am conscious, as I affirm and deny, that God is, and that is he what he is, in a mode of being that is infinite and, in the end, incomprehensible.

Thus, the Fathers carried the answers to the noetic and onomastic questions beyond the point where the Scriptures had left them. As a piece of systematic thought, however, their theology of the divine names was only inchoate. They did not fully explain how and why it is that the pale similitude between the world and God which is so completely overshadowed by the greater dissimilitude between God and the world can be made the starting point of a dialectic of understanding whose term is a true, though altogether imperfect, knowledge of the Unknowable. At that, their theology was adequate for its purpose, which was polemic and defensive rather than speculative or systematic. The patristic concern was to defend the scriptural faith not simply by reaffirming its paradoxical affirmations but also by seeking a deeper understanding of them so as to bring them into harmony. Until this latter, characteristically patristic, task was accomplished, the scriptural affirmations could indeed still be made, but in a vacuum of understanding that was dangerous, as the Eunomian impiety had demonstrated. In the things of God it is perilous to misplace either one's agnosticism or one's gnosticism. The risk is the loss of one's God, who is lost both when he ceases to be God, because no longer unknown, and when he ceases to be our God, because not known at all.

Only inchoate as a systematization, the patristic theology of the knowledge and names of God was nevertheless a complete achievement in the order of religious thought. The achievement consisted in the transformation of one paradox into another, with the result that each of them illuminated the other and both of them together cast light on the common truth that sustained their paradox. The biblical paradox, that God is at once unknown and known, was transformed into the theological paradox, that the knowledge of God is an ignorance. Cyril of Jerusalem summed up the patristic insight when he said: "In the things of God the confession of no knowledge (agnosia) is great knowledge (gnosis)." The transcendent truth that both paradoxes brought sharply into focus was that God is uniquely an object of knowledge because God uniquely is. "I am God, not man."

The Thomist Problem

In order to complete this historical survey of the problem of God, I must now deal briefly with the medieval elaboration of the initial patristic treatment. The figure in view is St. Thomas Aquinas. Admittedly, he was not the typical medieval figure. He was a man of the university, a man of the city. On the view of his contemporaries he was the innovator, not the traditionalist. Not surprisingly, the view applies to his treatment of the problem of God. The more typical medieval figure was the man of the monastery, the man of the countryside, and within the monastic tradition the problem of God was not the understanding but the taste of him. What the monk sought was the "savor of God." In this sense, Hugh of St. Victor, for instance, would be the more typical medieval figure. I touch here a whole new subject, only to put it aside. We shall stay with the man of the university.

Arius and Eunomius transposed the problem of God, each

of them a different aspect of it, from the plane of the religious existence to the plane of theological understanding. The patristic answer to Arius, which was canonized by the Council of Nicaea, and the patristic answer to Eunomius, which was sanctioned by inclusion in the tradition, were adequate to the respective problems as they were stated at the time. But they served to raise a new issue. It was the issue of the scientific systematization of these conciliar and patristic answers by the theological reason, that is, by the philosophical reason functioning under the illumination of the Christian faith.

The validity of this new issue had been implicitly affirmed by the Council of Nicaea. It established the statute of the ontological mentality and its mode of conception and statement within the high mysterious province of the Christian faith itself. By so doing, it implicitly established the statute of the philosophical reason and its processes of analytic and synthetic thought within the distinct and inferior province, problematical rather than mysterious, of theology. I mean here theology in the strict sense, that is, Scholastic theology, the centuries-old discipline that is concerned, not with the certification of the truths of faith, whose truth and certainty are warranted only by the Church, but with their systematic understanding insofar as this understanding—analogical, imperfect, and always incomplete—is accessible to the resources of reason. Anselm of Canterbury (1033–1109) is commonly called the Father of Scholasticism, since he was the first to pursue systematically the implications of the axiom, derivative from Augustine, *Fides quaerens intellectum,* faith seeking an understanding of itself.

In respect of our present subject, the achievement of Aquinas was that for the first time in history he effected the transposition of the problem of God into a state of systematic theological understanding. His instruments were a developed metaphysic of causality, an articulated gnoseology and psychology, and, above all, an adequately elaborated doctrine of the analogy of being. The achievement represented the culmination of centuries of collective thought, patristic and Scholastic. It was also the personal triumph of a uniquely penetrating intelligence.

The Nicene problem receives its definitive treatment in Questions 27–44 of the First Part of the *Summa theologica.* The issue is the ancient one, how is it that the Son who is from the Father, and the Holy Spirit who is from Father and Son, are equally with the Father the one God. Aquinas, however, does not reproduce the patristic argument. He begins where it terminated, with the dogmatic conception of the homoousion, and his precise question is whether the dogma is theologically intelligible, that is, in some analogical terms.

The insight of Augustine had first glimpsed the analogy. The human intellectual consciousness is somewhat like the divine intellectual consciousness, since man is the image of God. At the same time, the divine mode of consciousness is utterly unlike the human mode, since God is God, not man. Aquinas elaborates the analogy with the utmost finesse, and, using it as a unifying thread, he constructs a masterpiece of relentlessly systematic thought, flawless in its structure, finished with all subtlety in its details. I can say no more than this about it; no brief description could do it justice. The only point here is to illustrate the advance made by Aquinas over the work of the Fathers. The advance was along a different line. Their work had been to defend the affirmations of faith against the Arian errors, utilizing the resources of the Scriptures. His work was to pursue a systematic understanding of the faith that they had affirmed, utilizing the resources of reason illuminated by faith.

The more general problematic of God is wrought out in Questions 2–13 of the First Part of the *Summa.* The basic structure is constituted by the two interrelated pairs of questions that had lain in a different form beneath the text of Scripture and that reappeared in new form in the patristic era. Now the questions are explicitly stated for the first time in an organized systematic pattern.

The first question to be asked about God, as about anything else, Aquinas says, is the existential question, whether God is. To this question he devotes the three articles of Question 2. The third article contains the classic statement of the five ways whereby it can be known that God is. The argument then continues:

> Having answered the question, whether a thing is, the inquiry moves to the question, how the thing is; the purpose is to know what the thing is. In the case of God, however, we cannot know what he is; but we can know what he is not. Of him, therefore, we cannot ask the question, how he is; but we can ask the question, how he is not. Hence we shall inquire, first, how God is not; second, how he is known by us; third, how he is named (I, q. 3, proem.).

This statement of the problem of God seems so simple as to be entirely obvious. It requires some effort to realize that it took nearly ten centuries to work it out into this systematic form. The pattern of the problematic had always been there; in one form or another the four questions had always been asked. They are the questions that man must ask about God in one form or another. There are no other basic questions; all others derive from these. If you wish to argue the problem of

God, whether on the planes of the religious existence, theological understanding, or pure reason, you are obliged to argue it within this identical problematical structure, exquisitely discerned and stated with genially stark simplicity by Aquinas.

I shall not deal in detail with the substance of the argument he incorporated within this structure, but two general aspects of it require comment. Call them his agnosticism and his gnosticism or, to use the patristic terms, his agnosia and his gnosis.

First, throughout the whole of his probing inquiry into the problem of God, Aquinas' constant concern was to protect the mystery of the divine transcendence from prying scrutiny. He was not the Arian dialectician who, in Gregory Nazianzen's sarcastic description, discoursed on the generation of the Son as if he had been there as midwife. Aquinas was the Christian theologian. His thought was directed by a sense of the awesome biblical truth that God is the Holy One whose Name is ineffable. As a theologian he states this truth in metaphysical form: "One thing about God remains completely unknown in this life, namely, what God is" (Commentary on Romans, chapter 1, lesson 6). He states the truth so often and so uncompromisingly that some of his commentators have become a bit alarmed at the patent poverty of the knowledge of God he permits to man in this life.

He makes it utterly clear, of course, that we can answer the question of existence, whether God is, and whether he is wise, good, and so on. Hence we can make affirmations about God that are true and certain. This is indeed cardinal. It insures God's presence to us and our presence to him, for, unless we know that the Other is, we cannot say that the Other is-with us. On the other hand, Aquinas makes it equally clear that with the exercise of the primary act of intelligence, which is to make affirmations or judgments of existence, the capacities of human intelligence in regard to God are exhausted. We cannot go on to answer the question of essence in its positive form, what God is. We cannot positively understand the God whose existence we have affirmed. We cannot, as it were, crowd him into a concept; in his transcendence he escapes our concepts.

Aquinas does not pretend that his doctrine of the analogy of being does any more than rescue our discourse about God from sheer equivocation. It lets us know that, when we are thinking and talking about God, it is really about God that we are talking and thinking. It does not assure us that what we think and say about God is what God is. With his gnosticism of affirmation, Aquinas joins what Sertillanges has called an agnosticism of definition. To be a bit monotonous on the point, as Aquinas himself was monotonous, we can know that God is but we cannot know what he is. In the end, our presence to him, which is real, is a presence to the unknown: "to him we are united as to one unknown," says Aquinas.

The doctrine was not new. It was the echo, in another form of thought and language, of the awesome utterance in Exodus, "I shall be there as who I am shall I be there." The text had found an earlier echo in the patristic era in the paradox that the confession of no knowledge of God is itself the great knowing of him. The further achievement of Aquinas was that he exploited all the rational resources of a sophisticated ontology and an elaborate theory of knowledge to enforce the conclusion that all human knowledge of God ends in ignorance. Where the Bible and the Fathers had simply asserted that so it is, Aquinas demonstrated why it must be so. He transformed the paradox of Exodus, which had been paraphrased by Cyril of Jerusalem, into a state of systematic scientific understanding.

The biblical doctrine that God's creation is somehow like its Creator and Lord is transposed into the gnoseological technique of the first of the three ways of knowing God—the way of affirmation. The biblical doctrine that God is wholly unlike his creation is transposed into the second way, the way of negation. The biblical doctrine that God is God, not man, is transposed into the third way, the way of transcendence or eminence. As this third doctrine is decisive, so the third way is determinant. It determined Aquinas to a remorseless pursuit of the exigencies of the second way.

We must, he says, deny to God, remove from God, all similarity to the corporal and spiritual worlds as we know them. God is not what anything in these worlds is. In point of essence, God's unlikeness to the finite world is total. When we have done this work of denial, he goes on, "There remains in our minds only [the affirmation] 'that he is,' and nothing more. Hence the mind is in a certain confusion." Obviously. How can intelligence affirm that God is at the same time that it denies that he is what anything else that it knows is? But even this is not the end: "As the final step, however, we even remove from him this very 'is-ness,' as 'is-ness' is found in creatures. And then the mind dwells in the darkness, as it were, of an ignorance. It is by this ignorance, as long as this life lasts, that we are best united to God, as Dionysius says. This is the darkness in which God dwells." Thus the theologian echoes the prophet: "Truly thou art a God who hidest thyself, O God of Israel, the Savior" (Isaiah 45:15).

Perhaps a word of caution is needed here. For all his final agnosticism in what concerns the definition of God—the understanding of what he is—Aquinas demonstrated what the Fathers had implied, that the confession of our ignorance of God is not to be made effortlessly, at the outset of inquiry. In that case our ignorance would be a sheer absence of knowledge and not itself a mode of knowing. There is nothing more disastrous, as someone has said, than a negative theology that begins too soon. Ignorance of God becomes a true knowledge of him only if it is reached, as Aquinas reached it, at the end of a laborious inquiry that is firmly and flexibly disciplined at every step by the dialectical method of the three ways. This method not only governs the search for the supreme truth but also guarantees that the search will end in a discovery. There is a knowledge of God, as there is a way to it. There is a valid language about God, as there is a true knowledge of him. "As who I am shall I be there." The way of man to the knowledge of God is to follow all the scattered scintillae that the Logos has strewn throughout history and across the face of the heavens and the earth until they all fuse in the darkness that is the unapproachable Light. Along this way of affirmation and negation all the resources of language, as of thought, must be exploited until they are exhausted. Only then may man confess his ignorance and have recourse to silence. But this ignorance is knowledge, as this silence is itself a language—the language of adoration.

This first aspect of Thomist thought about God—its definitional agnosticism—may possibly seem congenial to the contemporary mind, if perhaps for the wrong reasons. But a second aspect is normally repugnant. I refer to Aquinas' gnosticism with regard to the existence of God as a truth of the rational order.

The whole structure and content of the first thirteen questions of the *Summa* are formally derivative only from the datum of all human experience, "I-with-the-others-in-the-world." Unlike the biblical problematic, which came down from heaven in a theophany, the Thomist statement rises up out of the earth-

ly soil of experience. Moreover, the mode of argument where-
with each of the four questions is met and answered is formally
philosophical. Behind both the position and the resolution of
the problem of God stands Aquinas' resolute and altogether
serene assurance that it is within the native powers of the
human intelligence, if it be trained in the discipline of philosophy, to make and to demonstrate the highest of metaphysical
affirmations—to posit and to prove the judgment that God is;
that it is further possible for reason to go on to articulate a
complex conception of what God is not—a conception that,
despite its negative form, is of positive cognitive value.

From all this, the contemporary mind, particularly within
the company of professional philosophers, somehow instinc-
tively draws back. Its inclination, on reading the lengthy argument of this section of the *Summa,* would be neither to agree
nor to disagree with it. More likely, the contemporary mind
would feel that in the intellectual climate that sustains such an
argument it can only gasp for breath. The fixed philosophical
attitude today is to say that a natural theology is impossible,
that it is impossible for human reason, beginning only with the
data of experience, to construct a valid doctrine of God, to
effect a purely rational resolution of the quadriform problematic. This philosophical disposition is furthermore the common Protestant theological disposition. A philosophy of religion is indeed possible but not a philosophy of God. Between
the order of rational affirmation and conception, which is the
order of philosophy, and the order in which the notion of God
is conceived and his existence affirmed, which is the order of
religious faith, an impassable gulf is fixed.

This contemporary conviction has most serious consequences.
If this great gulf exists between faith and reason, it follows

that the philosopher, who must stand by reason, should also stand for atheism. If the universe of reason and the universe of faith do not at any point intersect, it is unreasonable to accept any of the affirmations of faith, even the first, that God is. The atheist denial is the reasonable position.

This is the position against which Aquinas firmly stands in the opening questions of the *Summa,* both in the name of his faith and also in the name of his reason. There may be argument about the precise intention of the famous Article 3 in Question 2, where Aquinas outlines the five ways of answering affirmatively the question whether God is. There may also be argument about the import of the cryptic phrase in which Aquinas states the conclusion reached by the different ways: "and this is what all men understand by 'God' "; "to this all men give the name 'God.' " In any event, it is obviously within the intention of the five ways—and of the whole *Summa,* for that matter—to demonstrate that reason is not atheist, that atheism is not the reasonable conclusion from the data of common human experience, that the twin universes of faith and philosophy, distinct as universes of knowledge, are not utterly divorced, that their cardinal point of delicate intersection is in the crucial instant when reason affirms, what faith likewise affirms, that God is. The issue here, which is formally philosophical, is of vital religious import. It concerns the statute of reason in religion. If reason has no valid statute in religion, it follows that religion has no reasonable status in human life. Therefore it is unreasonable for a man to be religious. The reasonable man is the atheist.

"How odd of God/To choose the Jews." So runs the celebrated couplet whose lightness of humor does not cancel the seriousness of its statement of the initial mystery of the redemptive economy. A greater oddity, however, could be conceived. How odd of God it would have been had he made man reasonable so that, by being reasonable, man would become godless. This brings me to my third subject—that most mysterious of all the oddities on the face of God's earth, the godless man.

THE CONTEMPORARY PROBLEM:
THE DEATH OF GOD

I PREFER TO SPEAK of the godless man rather than of atheism in order to avoid any possible suggestion that the problem is abstract or that it presents an issue only on the level of argument. The suggestion would be entirely false. God is not a proposition but an Existence: "I am he who is." Similarly, godlessness is not a proposition but a state of existence. The knowledge of God is not an affair of affirmation alone; it is a free engagement in a whole style of life. Similarly, ignorance of God is not simply a want of knowledge or even a denial; it, too, is the free choice of a mode of being. All this will appear, I hope, as we go on. The point at the moment is that our present problem, like the problem of God, is concrete. Both problems may indeed be argued, and they must be, but their solution, like their origin, is not in terms of argument but of existence.

The problem of the godless man, like the problem of God, has its biblical form, and there I shall begin. The method will again be historical and descriptive as well as interpretative, that is, directed to an issue of theological understanding.

The Godless Man in the Bible

The Bible presents three major types of the godless man: the godless man within the people of God, the godless peoples outside the people of God, and the godless philosopher. All three are prototypes.

The first type is called by the Psalmist the "fool," the senseless man: "The fool says to himself: 'There is no God'" (Psalm 14:1). His meaning ought to be clear from what I have said about the existence of God as biblical thought understood it. The fool's denial does not concern God's existence in some metaphysical sense but his active existence in the midst of his people. The senseless man is saying to himself: "God is not here, now, with me." He is contrasted with the "man of sense" in the ensuing verse, the "man who seeks God" and actively recognizes his presence in the moment. More specifically, the fool's denial falls on the presence of God as his judge. He is the "stupid man," the "senseless man" of Psalm 92, who "knows nothing" and who "understands not at all" the terrible truth that, "if the wicked sprout like grass, and if evil-doers flourish, it is only to be destroyed forever" (92:7–8). The folly here is not innocent, a sheer vagary of the mind. The fool is the "wicked man" of another Psalm: "The wicked man applauds the desires of his soul; greedy for gain, the wicked man curses, renounces Yahweh [the God who is here]; high in passion, he does not seek him. 'God is not here!' This is his whole thought" (10:3–4). Behind the denial of God's presence as judge clearly lies the will to libertinage, to the passionate

78

existence as we might call it. Because I will that what I do be permitted, says the senseless man, therefore I deny that God is here to tell me that it is not permitted. The denial, like the will behind it, is senseless—a violation of religious intelligence, a sinful defect of moral quality.

The biblical fool is the prototype of the perennial godlessness of the people of God; he represents the archetype of the unbelief of believers. Of the people of God, Jeremiah's prophetic word, spoken in context of the house of Israel, is forever valid: "They have denied Yahweh; they have said, 'He is not [not Yahweh, not the Lord in their midst]'" (5:12). The denial is not of the theoretical order. It has the sense of an active ignoring of the presence of God, a refusal to abide his judgments.

The second type of the godless man in the Bible takes the form of the godless peoples. The phenomenon appears in the Old Testament. So Jeremiah, for example, speaks of "the peoples who do not know God" (10:25). It reappears in the New Testament. So St. Paul, for example, speaks of "the peoples who do not know the God [the Father] and will not listen to the good news of our Lord Jesus Christ" (2 Thessalonians 1:8). Outside the people of God are the people who are "godless in this world" (Ephesians 2:13). The concept "people" here bears its high biblical sense, which is religious and moral. The criterion of belonging or not belonging to the people of God is not racial descent, political allegiance, or even ritual practice. They are the people of God who know him, that is, "go with" him, realize their religious and moral relation to him by a life of faith and obedience.

Here we encounter the biblical analogous prototype of the massive contemporary phenomenon known as political atheism, the godlessness· of the polis, the people that, publicly as a people, are godless. Here, too, in the concept of the Two Peoples is the biblical analogue of Augustine's later conception of the Two Cities.

The godless peoples receive harsh judgment in the Bible. Their condition is painted in somber colors. In a word, they are in a condition of nonexistence. The judgment is to be understood in the light of the biblical conception of the knowledge of God. The people of God are constituted a people precisely by their knowledge of him, by their faithful, active recognition of his presence among them. This knowledge of God is the public philosophy or the social consensus that creates and sustains the political existence of the people. In the opening phrase of its implicit statement, "We, his people," the plural "we" has meaning and consistency only through the adjective "his." The historical existence of the people, as a social unity organized for action in history, gets its sense—its meaning and its direction—from the knowledge of God, with whose vitality all their temporal destinies are bound up. It follows in biblical thought that the peoples who do not know God have no principle of spiritual existence. They are in a state of nonexistence as peoples. They make no sense; their condition is absurdity. The condition is designated in the Bible by the symbol of darkness: the godless peoples "sit in darkness and in the shadow of death" (Luke 1:79). The New Testament text is a conflation of two texts from Isaiah, who joins with the image of darkness (the symbol of nonexistence) the image of a dungeon prison (the symbol of captivity).

This biblical theme of the Two Peoples is profoundly existential in some valid sense of that abused contemporary term. But it is also quite alien to contemporary ambient religious affectivity. So, perhaps, are the further biblical propositions that are allied to it and that sustain it. First, not to know the one God, living and faithful, is to be an idolater. Between the sharply drawn alternatives there is no middle ground. There is, for instance, no room for the third option of modern invention—an agnosticism more or less sophisticated, a skepticism more or less polite. Second, to be an idolater is to be an atheist. The prophets of the Bible show no tender disposition to seek out the belief that may be implicit in unbelief, nor are they inclined to be sympathetic with the religiosity of the irreligious, nor would they be willing to say, with men today, that there are no atheists but only idolaters. For the Scriptures the idolater is the atheist, and there is an end of it. From these two propositions the conclusion again follows that the idolatrous peoples are in a condition of absurdity.

From the eighth century B.C. onward, the prophets work out this conclusion in two steps. First, all the idols of the nations, whether they be the forces and phenomena of nature or the manufactured products of human art, are "nothingnesses," and their works are "nought" (Isaiah 41:24). They have no existence in the Hebraic sense, that is, no active existence, no power to save. As gods they are not even there. They are nullities, things of the void, absurdities. Second, the worship of idols nullifies the worshipper. "What they are," says the Psalmist, "those who make them will be, whoever puts his faith in them" (Psalm 115:8). The idolatrous peoples take on the condition of the idol which is impotence, emptiness, nonexistence. They are and they are not, which is absurdity. They inhabit the earth but they exist in the void. They are empty of the human substance, which is the knowledge of God. They are, if you like, the "hollow men" of Eliot's phrase. In the phrase of Isaiah, they are "lovers of ashes" (44:20) with no more solidity or cohesion than a heap of dust.

Moreover, they cannot plead, as an excuse for their idolatry, that they are simply ignorant of the one true God as they might be ignorant of some far continent to which no one from among them had ever voyaged. The single witness of St. Paul will serve here instead of many texts. He voices the whole Israelite tradition and reinforces its validity under the new dispensation when he writes from Corinth his serenely savage indictment of the idolatrous peoples whom he had encountered in his travels. "They are," he says, "without excuse" (Romans 1:20). They had refused the evidence that was before their eyes in the cosmos which is sacral in the sense that in it the "invisibilities" of God, his "eternal power and divinity, are clearly seen upon rational reflection." It was not just that they made a mistake; their fault was not of the intellectual order alone. Their idolatry was "impiety and wickedness" (1:18), a grievous fault of the moral order. They did not fall into idolatry; they made free choice of it, decided for it, gave deliberate preference to it. In Paul's cold language, "they did not see fit [or: intend] to have God in a true knowledge" of him (1:28). Their intention went elsewhere—to a "lie" over the "truth," to "the creature rather than the Creator" (1:25), to a god of their own making who would be present to them, powerless perhaps, but at least undemanding. So it happened that "they nullified themselves by their own arguments and their senseless mind plunged into darkness" (1:21). This did not happen by accident, inadvertence, sheer error. The issue had been one of intention, and it had been made clear to them: "What can be known about God was publicly knowable; for God himself had made it public knowledge" (1:19). The issue was therefore put to their freedom. This is why they were without excuse. Behind their idolatry lay not a misconception but a choice. In the end, they were godless in consequence of a will to godlessness.

This second type of the godless man, in the biblical form

of the godless people, was destined to reappear in history, as we shall see.

The third type of the godless man in the Bible was the godless philosopher. The Sage of Israel, who wrote in the tradition of Solomon and inherited his name, encountered him in the world of Hellenistic culture, late in the history of Israel. In the Book of Wisdom, the Sage describes the man of learning who explores the work of the Creator and fails to find the Creator himself. Instead he makes idols of the cosmic processes and powers. In so doing, of course, he makes his own learning the supreme idol. The Sage deals with the godless philosophers more gently than with the vulgar masses who bowed before statuettes and figurines. "It may be," he says, "that they but lose the way in the course of a search for God with a will to find him. Absorbed in his works, they strive to fathom them; but they let themselves be caught in outward appearances, so beautiful are the things that come beneath their eyes" (Wisdom 13:6–7). The Greek phrase of the Septuagint is exquisitely turned: *kala ta blepomena*. It is the eternal excuse that is no excuse.

These ancient scientists, ancestors of a long lineage today grown vast in number, were bemused and bewitched by the beauties and powers of nature, "fire and wind and the subtile air, the starry vault, the headlong flood, the lamps of heaven —upon these they look as upon gods, the lords of the world" (13:2). It may be, says the Sage, that "a lesser blame attaches to them" (13:6). At least they were engaged in the pursuit of truth; their error was to have idolized the pursuit itself. They do not, however, escape indictment: "In the end, even they are inexcusable. If they had the capacity to amass science enough to scrutinize the universe, how was it that they could not even more quickly discover the Master?" (13:8–9). God is not among the secrets of nature, to be discovered only by the laborious toil of science. He is indeed hidden but only so as to be "not far from any one of us," as Paul, depending on the wisdom of Israel, would later tell the Areopagus (Acts 17:27). Man, who is God's image, cannot fail to find God just below the surface of his works and accessible to ready inference, but man can refuse to recognize him. This is the folly with which the Sage charges the scientists. They are, he says, "utter fools" (13:1). For all their learning, they failed to grasp the first fact evident about the cosmos, that it is not God, that it is not divine, that it is, however, sacral, as the work of God which reveals its Artisan.

Here, in Egyptian Alexandria in the first century B.C., we find the analogous prototype of the godless philosophers and scientists of the modern age, to whom we shall later return.

This rapid survey of the biblical types of the godless man should serve to make clear the basic question in the matter. In the last analysis, is atheism an intellectual position reached by argument or a total option made by free decision? Is it simply a view of reality or a stance taken toward reality? Surely the biblical answer is unequivocal. The godless man, in any of his forms, is in bad faith (I can use the phrase almost in the sense of Sartre). His existence is not authentic. He refuses to recognize the reality of the human situation by refusing to recognize God, who is present in the situation, constituent of the whole meaning of the situation. The Bible clearly locates the ultimate root of atheism not in an erroneous judgment of the mind but in an act of choice, made somehow in the name of freedom, that launches the project of living the godless life. For this act, man is responsible. The biblical verdict is not doubtful. Thus to choose existence without God is to choose nonexistence. It is to fall into absurdity.

I might simply mention here that this biblical view of atheism has reappeared, with differences, in those post-modern philosophies whose basis is a postulatory atheism. Sartre, for instance, considers atheism to be the radical decision, the fundamental project. It is the original choice of one's self-in-the-world that is at the same time the discovery of the world, for the world from which God is absent reveals itself across the intention that he be absent. It is to the credit of Sartre's perspicacity that he does not even attempt to cast up a rational justification of the decision, the choice, and the ensuing project. They are by definition absurd. The will to be an atheist is the will to be a man, and to be a man is to strive to be God. This, the human project, is absurd, and it is chosen as being absurd. In a strange way, Sartre's view of atheism is hauntingly biblical. But this is to anticipate.

It is on the biblical view of atheism that I approach the problem of the godless man as he appeared in later history. The problem, therefore, is to discern the variant modalities of the will to atheism that lie at the root of the variant historical forms of atheism. Here, of course, the concern cannot be with any individual. In the individual case, the root of atheism, like the root of religious faith (or the roots of sin and virtue, for that matter) is ultimately ineffable. As the original act of freedom, the will to atheism, again like the will to faith, issues forth from the deepest regions of the self, where freedom is more than choice, where it is the self recognizing its own existence in the recognition of God or rejecting its own existence in the refusal of God—and thus lapsing into absurdity, since God, for all that he may go unrecognized, continues to belong to the structure of human existence. Therefore, I leave aside all individuals. On the other hand, I think it is possible, within the limits of valid generality, to discern and to understand the characteristic tenor and tonality of the will to atheism in different historical epochs. For the purposes of manageable discourse, I shall make a distinction—not substantially disputable, I think—between two major epochs.

The first begins in the quattrocento with the rise of what Lagarde has called *"l'esprit laïque,"* the laicist mentality; and it runs through the nineteenth century. Call this the modern age. The second epoch begins with Marx as its philosopher and with Nietzsche as its prophet, and it is still running on to an end not yet in sight. Call this, for want of a better term, the postmodern age. The two ages, of course, overlap in their courses, and neither had any absolute beginning. In fact, both terms designate not so much distinct divisions of historical time as different regions of the human spirit, diversely colored climates of the soul.

The Godless Man of Modernity

Given the exigencies of space, I must now rise, more reluctantly than Dr. Johnson, to the "grandeur of generality" and state a proposition with regard to the modern age. It reveals two types of the godless man. First, there is the godless man of the Academy, the bearer of the aristocratic atheism of the seventeenth and eighteenth centuries. The dynamic behind his atheism was the will to understand and explain the world without God, meaning by "world," nature, man, history, society. Second, there was the godless man of the Marketplace, the bearer of the bourgeois atheism of the nineteenth century. The dynamic behind his atheism was simply the will to prosper in the world without God.

I hasten to add that this is much too simple a view of the historical matter. It leaves out, for instance, the whole political

dimension. The aristocratic atheism of the French Enlightenment also embodied a political will. The attack on religion—
more exactly, on the Catholic faith and on the statute of the
Church in public life—had as one of its important purposes to
undermine the status of the king, to clear the way for a direct
attack on the absolute monarchy, which was supported by the
authority of the Church. Similarly, a political will lay behind
the bourgeois atheism of the nineteenth century. Across its
hostility to religion ran the intention of eradicating the rem-
nants of feudalism—the power of the Restoration monarchies,
the privileges of the nobility, the wealth of the great land-
owners—which, again, stood in close relation to the ecclesiastical order. In the seventeenth and eighteenth and even in the
nineteenth centuries, you could not touch religion without
touching politics and vise versa—just as then and later you
could not touch metaphysics without touching religion. Upon
the dissolution of the fragile and impermanent medieval synthesis, there had supervened a vast confusion of disciplines of
thought and realms of action. In a lamentable way the history
of modern atheism is intertwined with the history of the modern
liberties, as they were called. Perhaps it need not have been so,
but so it was. In any case, the political dimension of the problem of atheism is too complicated for any brief investigation.
Furthermore, it is, I believe, adventitious, the product of contingent historical circumstances. It does not illuminate the basic
problem which is essentially of the religious and intellectual
order. If there had never been a union of throne and altar, the
godless man of modernity would have arisen anyway.

The basic problem, I take it, is to account for the genesis
of the will to atheism characteristic of *l'esprit laique* and of
the modern age—the will to understand the world, or to make
a living in it, without God. Here we confront a lengthy task

in intellectual, cultural, and religious history. I must be content to point to the importance of one complex factor—I mean the medieval achievement. In the Middle Ages, three great intellectual events took place that were decisive for the history of atheism.

The first medieval event was the transposition of the problem of God into a problem for the philosophical intelligence, a formally metaphysical, gnoseological, and linguistic problem. For the first time in history the quadriform problem was squarely put to human reason. This was a daring thing to do. The exposure of the problem of God to rational inquiry was an invitation to betrayal of the tradition of reason. In the medieval period, the tradition of reason was considered a tradition of both faith and reason, within which the will to rational understanding harmonized with, and was sustained by, the will to Christian faith. Within the tradition so understood, therefore, reason refused to betray itself by running to atheist conclusions. The betrayal occurred when modernity chose to divorce the universes of faith and reason; in this choice, the modern will to atheism manifested itself. It was by this choice that the way was opened to the atheist conclusions of modern philosophy. This is the first aspect of the story; the second is closely related to it.

The second medieval event was the Thomist reception of Aristotle. Its effect, in regard of our present matter, was to introduce a view of the universe significantly different from the view fostered by the older Augustinian tradition, in which the universe was regarded chiefly as an arena in which man was to pursue his search for God, in his image and in his vestiges. The universe was *aliquid Dei,* something of God; its value lay in this alone. In the new Thomist view, the universe was a subsistent order of being, radically distinct from God, endowed with its own proper autonomy. It was therefore to be explored and explained by intelligence in terms of philosophical principles of being and the laws of rational thought. Biblical thought had de-mythologized the universe, expelling from it gods and demons and the whole host of demiurges. Aquinas extended the biblical insight, with the aid of Aristotle's formal materialism (if I may so characterize Aristotelian hylomorphism, the doctrine of the composition of material being out of matter and form). He transformed into systematic philosophical statement the biblical view of the world as an order of reality outside the order of the divine, revealing God indeed but not containing him. As it was itself a profane order, there was no profanation in searching out its secrets. No taboos stood in the way. Moreover, man, the image of God in virtue of his endowment with intelligence, was the appointed master of the world. Here again, however, in the medieval view of the world as the proper object of man's rational understanding, there lurked an invitation to betrayal of the tradition.

Scholasticism in the Thomist style did indeed authorize a mode of rational inquiry, philosophical or scientific, that was methodologically atheist. It did not start with God but only with experience. This inquiry, however, was conducted within the tradition of reason as the School understood it. Therefore, it was not the only mode of inquiry; the kind of truth it sought was not the only kind of truth; its techniques of certification were not the only ones available. Truth was a many-storied edifice. Lest the architectural metaphor be misleading, I should say rather that there was one universe of truth, within which different kinds of truth, and correspondingly different methodologies for their pursuit, existed in distinction and in unity. Moreover, in the Middle Ages, there prevailed the robust belief that between the valid conclusions of rational thought and the doctrines of faith no unresolvable clash could or should occur. The betrayal occurred when modernity, having divorced faith and reason, went on to decide that there is only one form of rational truth, one method for its pursuit, one measure of the certitudes attained.

In this decision, the modern will to atheism is more clearly discernible. Scientism supervened upon rationalism. If scientific methodology is atheist, as it is, and if it is the only methodology, as it is said to be, the mind has no way of reaching transcendental truth. There is, in fact, no transcendental truth. And there is no God. No evidence for his existence can be discerned by the methodology of science.

As long as modernity was faithful to its fundamental will, which was to explain the world without God, it did not greatly object to talk about God, under the proviso that the discussion was held outside the Academy, preferably outside all public places. There remained, however, the problem of explaining why there was such talk. More exactly, the basic modern project of explaining the world without God necessarily entailed the subordinate project of explaining God, who had for so long been associated in men's minds with the world. More bluntly, for the modern will to atheism, the problem was to explain God away. In the logic of modernity this was easily done. Since faith and reason are incompatible realms of the spirit, God can have nothing to do with the order of intelligence. He is therefore to be relegated to the order of fantasy. Religion is the work of imagination. By the nineteenth century, this had become the classic thesis of modernity. It is to be found everywhere in one form or another. As found in Marx, it serves to link this post-modern figure with the modern age.

The modern thesis wrought itself out most completely in the school of religious, philosophical, and historical thought that was most aptly christened modernism. The Christian position had been that Christianity is a religion of events; its faith is based on historical happenings. It is also a religion of dogmas; its faith is expressed in affirmations that are true and therefore bear on transcendental reality—on God himself and on his will for man. To the modern anti-intellectual spirit, this could only be pretentious nonsense—what the Marxist would call mystification.

On grounds of its own postulate, reduced to its logical extreme, modernity was obliged to say that Christianity is a religion of myths. The events on which it takes its stand never happened; they are simply the projection into history of man's experience of himself-in-the-world. As there never was a Sisyphus or any hill or stone, so there never was a Christ or any resurrection from the dead. Both myths fulfill the same function, which is to give an account of man's experience, whether of frustration in this world or of aspiration to a higher life. Both myths embody a sort of truth, but not a truth of the historical order. Neither states a fact; both state only fantasies. Moreover, as the Christian events are myths of no historical truth, so the Christian dogmas are symbols of no ontological truth. By no means do they have the absolute intellectual value of statements about the objective order of being, about God and his will. They have only the relative, pragmatic, emotional value of statements about the subjective order of religious experience. They do not translate into permanently valid affirmations the meaning of God's actions in history: there were no such actions. They merely translate, into some transiently appealing mode of pseudo-philosophical statement, my reactions to myself-in-the-world. These reactions are, in the end, the only religious reality. On both counts, therefore, as a religion of events and as a religion of dogma, Christianity is fantasy, the work of the imagination. To this conclusion, as to its destined end, the modern will to atheism ran. Talk about God, if you will, modernity said, but kindly remember that you are talking only about yourself.

The third great medieval intellectual event, the most significant of all, was the construction of the problematic of creation. This was conceived to be what it still is, the central problem of Christian philosophy—the problem of the coexistence and coagency of the infinite and the finite, the necessary and the contingent, the eternal and the temporal, the absolute and the relative. There were two aspects to the problem—one metaphysical, the other moral.

The metaphysical problem of God-and-creature is easily stated. If God is, and if God is what he is, how can anything else be? Outside the infinite, necessary, eternal, absolute being of God there seems to be no room for another order of being that is finite, contingent, temporal, relative. It was integral to the tradition of reason in the medieval sense to say that this is a problem of synthesis. The problem was the reconciliation of truths that stand to each other in an opposition not of contrariety but of polarity. Conceiving it as such, the Scholastics wrestled with it with no little success. But the statement of the problem was itself an invitation to betrayal of the tradition. Modernity succumbed. It decided to consider the problem as a choice between alternatives that really are contrary. In this decision and in the choices that flowed from it, the modern will to atheism declares itself in its full determination.

The alternatives are clear enough. You may decide to say either that God alone is, or that the world alone is. From both of these decisions, the consequence is atheism.

Suppose you decide to say that God alone is. It will follow that, since the world is there with all empirical obviousness, the world itself must be of the divine order of being. You thus choose pantheism in one or other of its forms. The most ancient form, primitive animism, is no longer a viable option, since to the modern it reeks of superstition. You may, however, choose to refine ancient Gnostic speculations into the less imaginative, seemingly more philosophical form of emanationist pantheism. Or you may opt for a dynamic pantheism, the theory of the emergent deity. Or your choice, inspired by the nineteenth-century exigence for system-building, may fall on some form of idealist monism; you may hold that only the Idea is the Real (God) and that all things else are but finite realizations of the Idea. In any case, you choose atheism, because pantheism is atheism. If everything is God, nothing is God. More exactly, pantheism is the denial of God as Creator, and, if God is not the Creator, he is not God. Here, I would note, the precise direction of the modern will to atheism appears with all clarity. It does not go against the sheer existence of God; it goes against the Christian affirmation that God is the Creator of the world.

On the other hand, you may decide to say that only the world is, that it is all there is or, at the very least, that it is all that matters. The material universe, man included, is a self-sufficient, self-contained entity and order. It subsists by itself, and it always has been there—from eternity, even. Somehow or other it managed to originate itself, if indeed there be any sense at all in speaking of its origination. In any case, it serves to explain itself. Beyond this world lies nothing. There is, first and last, no God. "The stars, she whispers, blindly run." With this, you have decided for materialism. It remains for you to choose the form of it. Ancient Stoic materialism is probably too much a piece of fantasy, too obviously unscientific, for the reason of modernity. In addition, its ethic was too sternly rational. You may, however, if you still belong to the earlier nineteenth century, choose mechanistic materialist monism. And you may update it a bit by the embellishment of a later evolutionism. In any case, your choice is atheism. The fact is patent, and it is usually acknowledged. Certainly it was acknowledged by the village atheist, that great nineteenth-century phenomenon for whom Haeckel, as completed by Darwin, was the Last Intellectual Word.

You may, however, find the high rationalistic optimism of the nineteenth century a bit passé. You may, with Marx, see the shallowness of materialist monism, especially of the mechanistic variety. You may therefore want to choose Marxist dialectical materialism. But in that case you must be careful—that is, if you still want to carry through the modern will to atheism. The issue here is complicated; I shall cheerfully make it simple. It is quite obvious, and it was openly admitted by Marx, that atheism is the postulate of dialectical materialism in the Marxist sense. It is not at all obvious, even though Marx did not admit it, that atheism is the conclusion of Marxist dialectical materialism. If this theory of reality is held to be only a philosophical-scientific theory; if it is therefore held to be open to further critical development, as all such theories are; if, that is, Marxist dialectical materialism is not transmuted, by the alchemy of a political will to an atheist society, into an immutable dogma as has happened in the Soviet Union; if all this is the case, it may well be that dialectical materialism is open to the theist conclusion. It may well be that it does not run inevitably to the atheist conclusion.

It may well be so, I say; there are scholars who say it is. For my part as a theologian, I am content to say that so it may be. For the rest, the issue is one of scholarship. The question is, what would an immanent critique of Marxist dialectical materialism reveal—that it is open to, or shut against, association with belief in God? The question is important today, but it is not my question here. My own proposition, derivative from the Bible, is that atheism is never the conclusion of any theory, philosophical or scientific. It is a decision, a free act of choice that antedates all theories. There are indeed philosophies that are atheist in the sense that they are incompatible with faith in God. But they are reached only by a will to atheism. This will, and the affirmation into which it is translated ("There is no God"), are the inspiration of these philosophies, not a conclusion from them.

There are, in general, two such philosophies, a pantheist monism and a materialist monism. More simply, there is only one such philosophy, a monistic philosophy. (It is not clear that dialectical materialism is a monism.) Behind monism lies the decision to transform the medieval problem of synthesis, God-and-creature, into the modern problem of choice, God-or-creature. This decision was not reached by argument; it represents the will to atheism, the mark of the spirit of modernity.

These two philosophies, which are radically one, are the pure positions. There remains the impure position, which is less a position taken by intelligence than a paralysis of intelligence itself. You may opt for the *epoche* of the contemporary phenomenological school, that is, for a systematic suspension of judgment in the face of all ontological or metaphysical questions. This school of thought will describe with great fineness the "situation," what is there to be observed, outside man and inside him, but it will not make judgments of existence. It declines the use of the formidable verb "is" in affirmations. If you retire to this school, you will have simply to refuse altogether the problematic of God in its Thomist mode of statement. The first question, whether God is, will stop you. It is the kind of question that you do not deal with on principle. Your position will be a metaphysical agnosticism, a sort of Eunomianism in reverse.

It may be asked whether this agnosticism is not a lower form of atheism than idolatry. The idolater does not hesitate to affirm that God is. On the witness of the Sage of Israel he is in search of God, not doubting that God can be found. Only then does he go astray, and his error is with regard to the second question, what God is. His error is inexcusable, but perhaps the Sage would say that he merits less blame than the modern agnostic. The latter, incidentally, is a phenomenon the Sage apparently never met. In the wisdom literature of Israel, one does indeed find the world-weary skeptic, but his temper of mind is quite different from that of the modern agnostic. This latter breed says in effect that, since he cannot know what God is, he will refuse to affirm that God is. But this stupidity, one may well think, surpasses that of the idolater. It is not merely an implicit refusal of God; it is an explicit denial of intelligence. The essence of God does indeed lie beyond the scope of intelligence, but his existence does not. This is a truth, the Sage of Israel would say, that any man ought to know. It is the first among the truths that no man is allowed not to know, for not to know it is to nullify oneself as a man, a creature of intelligence.

Agnosticism is atheism by default. The agnostic gives up even the search for God. He calls an arbitrary halt to the movement of the mind that, as Paul told the Areopagus, is native to it. This movement is indeed a "groping," Paul said (Acts 17:27), but, he adds, it should not fail to end in a grasping. God is not beyond reach; he is "not far from anyone of us." Agnosticism is also an atheism of despair. The search for God, says the agnostic, is too perilous for me; it is beyond my powers. In this willful diminution of intelligence, God disappears. Surely this is a miserably flat dénouement to the great intellectual drama in whose opening scene Plato appeared with the astonishing announcement that launched the high action of philosophy—his insight that there is an order of transcendent reality, higher than the order of human intelligence and the measure of it, to which access is available to the mind of man.

The foregoing analysis of the aristocratic atheism of modernity reveals two characteristics.

First, it gives the appearance of being a conclusion of reason: "Therefore there is no God." The appearance, however, is deceptive. Behind the seeming rationality of the conclusion lies the dynamism of a radical decision for which no rational justification can be offered. Only in virtue of an original act of freedom, the will to atheism as a project, could the atheistic conclusion have appeared. The decision was to make a separation where the tradition had made only a distinction—between faith and reason. The order of faith, said modernity, is as separate from the order of reason as the order of fantasy is from the order of the idea, as separate as the order of myth is from the order of fact. The further decision was to postulate a univocity where the tradition had proved analogy in the order of truth as it is related by the manifold powers of intelligence to the order of being. There will be only a single truth, said modernity, not a unity of truth. The final decision was to posit a dichotomy, God or the world, where the tradition had proposed a synthesis, God and the world. In these fateful decisions, and not in any process of argument, the root of the atheism of the modern Academy is to be found.

Second, the full verbal formula for this atheism runs thus: "Because we have no need of God in order to understand and explain the world, there is no God." Here the modern project comes to view more clearly. This is what modernity willed to do—to explain the world without God. The fundamental refusal had fallen on the "God of explanation," as he was called, though his proper Name is the Creator, the Craftsman of the Book of Wisdom (13:3), who is also He Who Is, without whom nothing is intelligible because without him nothing is.

The essence of the modern matter appears in the famous interchange between the great astronomer, Pierre Simon Laplace, and his friend Napoleon, then First Consul. On its appearance in 1796, a copy of Laplace's *Exposition du système du monde,* a book destined to make history, was presented to Napoleon by its author. After reading it, Napoleon complimented his friend. This explanation of the world, he said, is admirable. "But," he added, "I find in the book no mention of God." Laplace replied, in a sentence that contains the distilled essence of the atheism of the modern Academy, "Je n'avais pas besoin de cette hypothèse."

The formula also states the point of similarity between this aristocratic atheism and the later bourgeois development characteristic of the nineteenth century. In the Marketplace, said *les gens de bien* (whether they spoke French, English, or any other vernacular), we have no need of God; therefore he does not exist. The project of these men was not to explain the world but simply to make a living in it. To them the sole realities of life were economic. The business of business is business, they might have said (the lapidary axiom was operative long before it was coined). And to the business of business, God is irrelevant. He is not needed for the success of the economic enterprise, which is the only enterprise that matters.

There is hardly need to delay over this atheism of distraction. Perhaps its chief significance is that it served to posit the problem of God in the popular terms of economic and social fact and endeavor rather than in the aristocratic terms of philosophy and science. It further served to prepare the way for the later proletarian atheism, the "apostasy of the masses," as Pius XI called it, and their atheism of indifference. This was the more decisive nineteenth-century event, since it was the matrix of Marxism.

Before leaving the modern age I must at least briefly mention another type of atheism that it brought forth. It was an atheism of the City, the political atheism that went under the pseudonym of anticlericalism. It was inherent in the political theory of *l'état laique,* which issued from the Enlightenment and the Revolution, though it had roots much farther back. Its twin postulates, the dogma of the indivisibility and omnicompetence of state sovereignty and the dogma of separation of church and state, came to fullest expression in the Third French Republic and the Law of Separation of 1905. The modern will to atheism thus made its way into the City as well as the Academy and the Marketplace. It inspired the politico-religious dogma that was the main structural rib of the laicist state—the dogma that religion is a purely private matter, an affair of the inner forum, a concern of the individual conscience. At best, religion belongs "in the sacristy" (as the phrase went), the ecclesiastical forum that is, by laicist dogmatic definition, a private forum. The dogma decreed that God and religion can claim no public status, no place in the public forum, no function in the public action of the state. Public life is by definition godless. The concept of a public religion is a contradiction *in adiecto.* So, too, is the concept of the people of God. The people, like the polis, are officially atheist. Atheism is the public philosophy, established by law. The establishment was accomplished by the law of separation of church and state, which was the legal institution that embodied the laicist politico-religious dogma. The law decreed that the church has no public existence within the state. The church is legally not present; it has no existence before the law; it may have no public activity. In effect, there is no church. The Temple of God was overthrown by legal fiat. God might still, if he liked, dwell in the individual heart. He was not to be allowed, however, to dwell in the midst of the people. The people, as such, do not recognize him; they do not acknowledge his presence. They say, "He is not here, in public."

Thus the nineteenth century saw the reappearance in a new form of the biblical phenomenon of "the people who do not know God." This was the atheism of the City against which Pius IX spoke in the Syllabus of Errors and against which Leo XIII directed a long series of encyclical letters. It was a phenomenon of transition. In one sense, it still belonged to the modern age, since its original premise was that the state has no need of God in its public life. God is irrelevant to politics—the assertion is typically modern. In three other senses, however, the political atheism of the French republics and of their continental imitators made a bridge to the post-modern age.

First, the political will to atheism took the form of a refusal of the God of history, the Political Craftsman who created a people, who dwells in their midst, who rules their destinies as Pantokrator. This was new. The earlier modern refusal had fallen on the God of the world, the Cosmic Craftsman whose work was the heavens and the earth. The new atheism or, more concretely, the new godless people who refuse to recognize the Pantokrator, would be characteristic of the post-modern age. Second, the totalitarian democracy that issued from the En-lightenment and the Revolution as the bearer of a new type of political atheism was, precisely in respect of its atheism, the lineal ancestor of the Communist totalitarian dictatorship that issued from Marxism and the world revolution as the bearer of a messianic atheism such as history had never seen. Third, the atheism of the City that modernity brought into being went beyond modernity in that it was more than a view of reality. Clothed with an armature of power by its incorporation in a state, it was a historical force that powerfully and quite consciously altered not only political reality but also the whole range of reality included in the concept of civilization. This too, would be the characteristic of post-modern atheism on the Marxist model.

The Godless Man of the Post-Modern Age

Two types of the godless man have appeared. Both are new. Their appearance is, in fact, the main reason why our own day needs a new name. "Post-modern" is not fully descriptive; but perhaps it sufficiently suggests the idea of continuity amid difference.

First, there is the godless man of the communist world revolution. He is not an individual, but a collectivity, a class, or better, a party, the creator of a people who will exhibit in finished form the biblical reality of "the people who do not know God." The dynamic of his atheism is not that of his modern predecessor—the will to understand and explain, without God, the given world that man immediately encounters distinct from himself. The new Marxist man wills to transform the world. By "world" he means all that Marx meant by "nature," that is, the total system of material production and human relationships that the labor of man has brought into being throughout history. The world is the industrial world, the world wrought by man's industry. Nature in this sense is man's "inorganic body," in Marx' phrase. With it man makes a unity; he is not wholly distinct from it, since it is his own work. Thus, it represents him or, better, it presents him to himself, and to that extent it is himself. In the course of its elaboration, man's inherent powers come to his view. Through this nature, which is his own work, man comes to concrete existence. The Marxist will is to transform the nature of man in this complex sense. And the transformation is to be effected not only without God but in his despite. In a word, which is Marx' own blunt word, the Marxist will is the "suppression of God."

Second, there is the godless man of the Theater. I call him such, using the word "theater" in much the same sense that it had for Bacon when he listed as his fourth set of human idols —more abstractly, prejudices—the "idols of the theater." I understand Theater, as he substantially did, to be the world of the public imagination, common impressions, generally shared feelings about things. It is essentially a world of dramatic fantasy and emotion which serve, however, as vehicles of ideas. Our new godless man inhabits the Theater in this sense after having himself created it. Its creation is his project, which he carries out largely through the media of art—the novel, preferably the play (in what already has its name, the "theater of absurdity"), painting, sculpture, and, even, the performing arts. He is not a philosopher in the high classic sense or even in the diminished modern sense. He cares nothing for metaphysics or epistemology, the quondam ally but modern enemy of metaphysics. His profession is phenomenology, the work of describing the "situation" of man. He would like to go on to ethics, but he has so far been unsuccessful in constructing an ethic other than an "ethic of the situation," which is not an ethic at all. In any case, he will not go on to anthropology if by this term is meant the science that deals with the nature of man. His postulate is that man has no nature; man is not an essence. Man is only a presence, a sort of process, or, if you give the word something of its primitive Hebraic sense, an existence, a continual "standing forth," an actual "being-there-in-the-moment" in action and in freedom.

The will of the godless man of the Theater is not that of his predecessor of the Academy—the will to understand and explain the world without God. For him the world is absurd. Still less does he will to change the world; for it would still be absurd no matter what the change. His project is simply to "exist" the godless world (I should spell the word "ex-sist" in order to bring out its transitive sense). Even more exactly, his project is to "exist" himself, the man who wills to be godless in a world that he sees to be godless through his intention that it should be godless like himself. He wills the absence of God.

What follows is an essay in characterization of post-modern atheism in its two typical forms. I shall first set down the traits that the two post-modern godless men have in common despite their many differences. I shall then comment briefly on the proper characteristics of each.

There are six characteristics that the man of the Revolution and the man of the Theater share. Singly and together, they identify these men as belonging to an age—or a climate of soul—that is not modern, though it exhibits a certain continuity with modernity.

In the first place, the two men share a common problematic. I said above that the Hebraic and Christian affirmation, God-and-the-world, gives rise to two problems. The metaphysical problem, which the medieval mind had wrought out into a philosophical mode of statement and resolution, chiefly preoccupied modernity. It was the problem of the coexistence and coagency of Creator and creature. The second problem, which has always claimed anguished attention, has now come into the foreground for a variety of historical and theoretical reasons over which we cannot delay. It is the moral problem. If God is, and if he is what he is, not only the Creator but the Pantokrator, how can the world be what it is, a place of manifold evil, an arena of human misery?

No man escapes this problem. It is put as a test to every man as it was put to the Israelites at Massah or Meribah amid the misery of a desert thirst. The test is not put to man's intelligence, for, unlike the metaphysical problem, which admits a manner of philosophical resolution, the problem of evil utterly defeats philosophy. The test is put to man's freedom. The temptation is to reject the reality of God's presence in the world as its benevolent and provident ruler in the rejection of the evil that is present with such dreadful reality. Man's questions here are not philosophical but historical-existential: "Where is my God? Is he the living God, or not?" This is the problem which the man of the Revolution and the man of the Theater confront, each in his own mode and mood.

In the second place, and in consequence, both men accept the myth of the death of God. It is a nice question to ask just why Nietzsche announced what he called his "dreadful news" and just what he meant by the news: "This old God is really no longer alive; he is thoroughly dead" (thus in one of many texts, this one from *Also sprach Zarathustra*). In any case, the myth is not a coinage of the modern age. In those days men were content to say, under comfortable pretense of rationality, that God does not exist, that is, his existence is not a truth of reason and therefore never was a truth at all but only a fantasy. The universe of reason, which is man's decisive universe, can do without it. In contrast, the myth announces a fact of history, a change in the whole course of events, a new direction for man's destiny. The myth is therefore fraught with passion, whether flaming rage, icy despair, or mad rejoicing. Therefore, too, it is a summons to decision. Whatever reason or faith may say or refuse to say about God's existence, the fact is that he is gone from history, and history is man's decisive universe, an arena of action. In his myth, Nietzsche consciously brought to terrible explicitness the question that the modern age had been able to avoid, though in bad faith. You may say, if only because men have said, that the world does not need a Creator to explain it, but you cannot say, because no one dares to say, that the world does not need a Ruler to govern it. If God is dead, who is the Pantokrator? Not even through bad faith can you avoid this question. It is the question that the man of the Revolution and the man of the Theater squarely confront, each in his own way, both standing on the common ground of God's death.

In the third place, and again in consequence, the new atheism of the Revolution and of the Theater is a postulate. It does not even bother to clothe itself in the guise of a conclusion from argument. In this respect it is more honest than the modern Academy ever was. Moreover, by its frank appearance as a postulate, an original free decision that is not disguised as a dialectical necessity, the new atheism reversed the positions of the forces in the field. The men of the Academy felt themselves obliged to make the case against God, against belief in him, against the ancient reasons for believing. The tradition was still in possession; it was thesis, the consensus. Atheism was innovation, antithesis, the dissent. The Enlightenment admitted as much by its contrast between *les préjudices* and *les lumières*. The positions hitherto prevailing are now reversed. Atheism becomes the postulate. The myth of the death of God is in possession; it is the thesis. If the antithesis is to validate itself, it is up to the Christian to bring God back to life, if he can. It falls to belief to make the case for itself.

I should add here that contemporary postulatory atheisms consider that modernity really made the case against belief. This is certainly true of Marx. Here and there he argues in the vein of the Academy—against the notion of creation, for instance. He only succeeds in making it clear to his reader that he did not even understand the state of the question. For instance, he confuses the problem of the duration of the world with the problem of its contingency. For the greater part, however, he is content simply to accept the proposition, which he took immediately from Feuerbach, that religion is fantasy, that God is the creation of man's own imagination. This, we saw, is the modern proposition. Even at that, Marxist atheism does not look back to this proposition as to its foundation. Neither does the atheism of the Theater. Neither of them looks back at all, certainly not to any of the arguments of the past when they seek warrant for their will, respectively, to the suppression of God and to the absence of God.

In the fourth place, the man of the Revolution and the man of the Theater agree in considering God to be not simply a needless superfluity to be dispensed with and disregarded but a positive menace to be actively combatted and done away with. God is a pernicious fantasy, not a harmless one. These two men are not content to be god-less; both are God-opposed. They hold, not for a-theism but for anti-theism. To each of them, God, Creator and Pantokrator, is the enemy. Hence the will to the suppression of God or to the absence of God.

In the fifth place, the two new God-opposed men base their active hostility to God on the same one general ground. As the Craftsman of nature and the Master of history, God is the enemy of man's freedom. As long as God is there, either to make man or, especially, to rule him, man is not free. The two men differ widely in their conception of freedom, but, for all their differences, they agree that freedom is absolute autonomy or it is not freedom. It is independence that is itself transcendent of all limits. If it be transcended and therefore limited by a divine freedom, it perishes. Man must be the god of his own world whether it be the world of Marxist nature or the world of theatrical absurdity. Otherwise man is not man.

In the sixth place, the Revolution and the Theater have in common, however much they differ in its description, a highly concrete concept of freedom. Neither of them is concerned with what modernity called freedom, the so-called modern liberties, the rights of man and citizen, the civil liberties that law can guarantee. Not by these paltry legal means is man's true liberation to be accomplished. They fail even to touch the problem of freedom. Endowed though he may be with the full panoply of the modern liberties, man is still a slave. To what? To his nature, say the two new men in chorus, though each uses the word in his own special sense. Man must be freed from his inorganic, still unorganized body through its organization in the communist society, says the Revolution. Man must be freed from his essence through an existence (in the transitive sense) into absurdity, says the Theater. In both cases the freedom is not a thing of ideas or laws; it is a thing of action and history. In neither case is it a matter of guaranteeing a freedom that is somehow given. In both cases it is a matter of creating a freedom that is not yet given. When they aim, as they do, at the liberation of man, both the Revolution and the Theater are aiming at the creation of man, a new creation whose condition is the suppression of God or the absence of God.

I should like now to make a series of comments on the God-opposed man of the communist world revolution. My single purpose is to illustrate the fact that he is a new phenomenon in history.

In the first place, the Marxist will to oppose God is not founded on some personal will to libertinage as in the case of the biblical fool, nor again on some prideful will to worship only reason as in the case of the modern *philosophes.* Marxist atheism has it roots not in the world of ideas but in the world of fact—in the social fact of human misery. It is an atheism of exasperation directed against the historical condition of man in the industrial age. At the bottom of an atheism whose matrix is the problem of evil, there lies a moral absolute. It asserts not only that evil has no right to exist but that its existence is intolerable. This is a principle of such absoluteness that the God of the Bible does not admit it as an imperative on his governance of the world. He judges evil to be evil, but he does not regard it as intolerable. He shows toward it the "forbearance" of which Paul speaks (Romans 3:25). This now becomes the charge against him. He who is God—so runs the indictment—ought not to tolerate evil. Since the God of the Bible does tolerate it, he is not God. God is rejected in the name of God himself. This is the purest and most passionate form of atheism, when man rejects God in the name of his own more God-like morality. It towers high above the petty biblical atheisms and above the shallow monisms of philosophy. Marxist atheism rises toward, if it does not reach, this height of purity and passion.

In the second place, out of the Marxist exasperation at the misery of man is born the will to freedom. Berdyaev somewhere tells the story of the Russian student in Paris who was asked, when he was about to leave the country, what his chief impression of France had been. In France, he replied, there is no freedom. This astonishing reply measures all the distance that lies between the modern and the Marxist concepts of freedom. For the Marxist, true freedom is the empowerment to alter nature, to transform man and society, to build a new world, to inaugurate a new history. This empowerment descends upon man through his recognition of the necessities inherent in the materialist dialectic of history. By this recognition man becomes the master of history. Precisely in this mastery, exercised in each concrete moment of history, man's concrete freedom consists. It is the freedom of the Pantokrator, an actuality of power over the historical process. By this freedom the man of the Revolution will make sense out of history, that is, give to it a new substance of meaning and impart to it a new direction toward the goal of a world without misery.

In the third place, the ultimate enemy of freedom in the Marxist sense is God, the Pantokrator. The knowledge of God in the biblical sense is the primary source of man's alienation. This Marxist concept is complex. For our purposes here it may be sufficient to say that the state of alienation is the contrary of the state of freedom. More exactly, because in more dynamic terms, alienation divests man of his freedom. The man who believes that God is the Pantokrator falls captive to an illusion. By fiat of the Marxist will, if not by deliverance from modern philosophy, God is an illusion. God is no more than man's own creation, the "sigh of the oppressed creature," in Marx' phrase (in the famous passage in which he calls religion the "opium of the people"). For the sake of his own comfort man projects into an illusory heaven the fantasy of a power who is master of history, powerful enough to rescue man from misery and to guide history to a paradise beyond history. But this is the projection of what man himself is. Therefore the projection, the fantasy projected, and the belief in the fantasy are utterly pernicious. They are man's alienation from himself.

Through belief in God, man becomes a stranger to his true self; he is paralyzed in his essential power, which is to be himself the Pantokrator. He is rendered impotent to do his historical work, which is to transform his nature and to organize the inorganic body that presently weighs him down in slavery under the conditions of misery characteristic of capitalist society, as formerly of feudal society.

Therefore the knowledge of God is to be eradicated from the midst of the new people of the Revolution. Moreover, the suppression of God is to be total, from private as well as from public life. Marx and his heirs were not deceived by the vacuous slogan of the modern godless man, that religion is a purely private affair. They had the genius to see that religion, even in the form of private faith, is the most public of all public affairs. Therefore, in the ideal Marxist society, no one is to be permitted to say, even in the privacy of his own heart, "God is here; the Pantokrator is living, active, in this moment." Such a man would be the fool, an apostate from the Revolution, whose whole success depends on the suppression of God, on the destruction of the belief that God is the Master of history. Lenin, the heir of Marx, is more explicit than his master on this crucial point. It may be, he said in 1905, that the state can choose to regard religion as a purely private affair; this is no more than a matter of tactics, a concession to the bourgeois spirit of the modern age. But for the party of the socialist revolutionary proletariat, religion is by no means a purely private affair. It is an affair of ideology; therefore it is an affair of the party; therefore it is a public affair. The struggle against religion is central in the ideological struggle. The propaganda of atheism is essential to the propaganda of the party. There is no room in the party for the Christian, for the man who believes that God is the Pantokrator, here, with us, in this moment of history, and there will be no room for him anywhere when the party comes to victory in the victory of the revolution.

In the fourth place, the myth of the death of God is integral to the ideology of the Revolution. Only it is not a myth. More exactly, under the literary form of myth, there lies a scientific fact. The fact is that the man of the Revolution has come to a scientific understanding of history. He has discovered the meaning of history. He has discovered that it is history, not God, that makes the nature of man. This discovery was the death of God. When man came to know himself through history, when he came to understand that he is the creature of history and not of God, God was dead. He died out of history, leaving man as its master.

In the fifth place, the God-opposed man of the Revolution is a new phenomenon by virtue of the scope he envisages for his historical work. His goal is nothing less than the solution of the problem of evil.

He understands what is true—that no solution to the problem is acceptable to man unless it is practical, that is, unless it means the actual deliverance of man from evil. Hence he undertakes this practical task. Moreover, he understands, what also is true, that the problem of evil can receive practical solution only at the hands of one who has the power to bring good out of evil. In the biblical tradition, this power is uniquely the prerogative of God. The Pantokrator can show forbearance toward evil in the world only because he can somehow make it serve unto the "vindication of his justice" (Romans 3:26). The man of the Revolution is more than ever such in that it is he who assumes this prerogative. It is the ultimate basis of the ethic of the Revolution. Evil may be permitted—in fact, evil may also be deliberately done—provided that it serves the cause of the Revolution. Out of present misery, permitted or inflicted, the new master of history can bring good.

The practical resolution of the problem of evil will be accomplished on the advent of the world-wide communist society, when the saving justice of the God-opposed man will have its vindication. The biblical history of salvation, which began when Yahweh became the living God who came down to rescue his people from the misery of their enslavement in Egypt, looked to a consummation that was at once a reality and a symbol—the entrance into the Land flowing with milk and honey. The new history of salvation, which began when the living God died in the historical discovery that he is not man's Creator and much less his Savior, also looks to a consummation that is, however, to be only a reality and not a symbol. The new master of history, the Party, renews the ancient promise to lead the people to the Land. Only now the Land is within the confines of this earth, and entrance into it will take place in time. The symbols of milk and honey are still valid; there will be abundance for all. But over the whole Land and all its people a new banner will fly, reminiscent of the one that Moses set up after Joshua's victory over Amalek, except that it will read: "God is not here; God is dead."

In the sixth and final place, the man of the Revolution displays a newly sure confidence, proper to the sovereign dignity that he has assumed. He is not, of course, a Condorcet, full of the bright and brittle confidence of the earlier rationalism that trusted to the shining of *les lumières* to dissolve *les préjudices.* Marx said: "Ideen können überhaupt nichts ausführen." And his heirs have taken him at his word. They have furnished Marx' new lights with an armature of power, in the form of a great state whose full resources are enlisted in the furtherance of the Revolution. They fully understand the uses of force in support of ideas. Again, the new man is no Comte, satisfied to believe that history itself will usher in the new age of science, terminating and replacing the ages of philosophy and theology. The new man knows that history, which needs a master, also needs a servant who will do its work. This is his supreme dedication—to be the servant of history. In this service he finds the deepest root of his confidence. He is the *contrefaçon* of the Servant of Yahweh of whom Deutero-Isaiah sang. He is self-less. He is incorruptible by money or pleasure. He is committed to the asceticism of constant work, the essential work of the working class, which is to hasten the consummation of the Revolution. Presently he wills to seize dictatorship over all the world, but only in order that he may thereby save the world. He even wills his own death, which is the withering away of the state, the instrument of his power, in order that this death may be the ransom of the Many, who will thus rise, by its virtue, to the new life of the classless society. This event is invisible now, but he confidently sees it coming. The invisible is always visible to faith.

This characterization concludes on a somewhat mystical note, deliberately struck. I think that the God-opposed Man of the Revolution is not fully understood unless the note of his mystique is heard.

It is much more difficult to characterize the second type of post-modern atheism represented by the new man of the Theater. He has come upon the scene much more recently; therefore his intentions are not so fully manifest. Moreover, one cannot speak of him as one can of the Marxist man, who presents, so to speak, a single face with lineaments that have settled into fixed lines, as happens with a man of some age and maturity who is set on a career. The man of the Theater is many men, all of them individuals, who do not look entirely alike, and it is difficult, if not impossible, to sketch his portrait. The model for him would probably be Jean-Paul Sartre, even though other men of the Theater would disclaim resemblance. In an odd, inverted way, Sartre is a Scholastic. He stands to the prophecy of Nietzsche as the Scholastic stood to the prophecy of the New Testament. The School, headed by Anselm, began with the axiom, "Credo ut intelligam," I believe in order that I may understand. The Scholastic question was, is what faith affirms intelligible? Sartre begins with the myth of the death of God. It is apparently his one article of faith, accepted as true without question. His question then is Scholastic, whether what faith affirms is intelligible. To be exact, I must change a word in the question. The word "intelligible" would doubtless not be intelligible to Sartre. He would not use it; it would not express his intention. He is a Scholastic with a difference. Properly stated, his question is whether what faith affirms, that God is dead, is livable. His intention is to "ex-sist" the death of God, to make to "stand forth" the world out of which God has died, to make a phenomenological description of the man from whom God is absent. In some such terms, the general intention of the man of the Theater, on the model of Sartre, may be stated. The statement needs nuance, which will be supplied, I hope, as I now venture to generalize.

In the first place, the original ground from which the man of the Theater proceeds is not in the world of ideas but in the world of fact. Before him at the outset is the problem of evil. He sees the world as Camus (himself no Sartre in temper or intention) saw it in *L'homme révolté*. What he sees is a circumscribed garden surrounded by death, and, beyond death, nothing. Death constantly makes incursions into the garden in the many forms that human death can take. There are the public forms of insensate war and the cruelty of concentration camps, the products of tyranny or folly in politics. There are also the private forms of innocence abused, loyalty betrayed, love soiled, honor traduced, failure, defeat, disease. The man of the Theater views this tragic spectacle not with cynicism but with compassion for man, who stands under such great menace from all sides. His climate of soul is the antithesis of that of the modern man for whom *les lumières* shone so brightly. His mind is full of darkness; it is oppressed with a sense of the finitude and fragility of existence; it shivers before the unpredictabilities of history. This post-modern man lives in a climate of anguish and anxiety.

In the second place, it does not occur to the man of the Theater that he should seek to understand and explain the world of his vision. He simply summons out of his vision the will to freedom. His concept of freedom is complicated and obscure. For our limited purposes here, say that it is man's will to be the "inventor of himself" (in Sartre's phrase). The will is heroic, but not in the old romantic style. The will is that man should recognize the absurdity of the world and that he should also recognize himself to be absurd. Man is not an essence; that is, in the depths of him there is no intelligibility, no structure of meaning. Man has no nature; that is, in the depths of him there is no ordered set of dynamisms out of which he might act with purpose and coherence. As it is with man, so is it with the world—the dramatic human world of history, with which alone the Theater is concerned. Let all this be recognized. Let there be no will to change it. Freedom is not the possibility of changing the world, as with the Marxist. There is no such possibility. The world is darkness, says the Gospel, uttering a stable, transtemporal truth. The world is absurd, says the man of the Theater, translating into sheer enigma what the Gospel understood to be only mystery.

The matrix of the human project is therefore given. And in this situation the radical decision is for freedom. For a man to be free is for him to assume single and full obligation for his own existence. It is for him to bear alone the entire responsibility for being. In the face of the world's absurdity, man's original choice is to be-for-himself. His project is to rescue and recover and realize himself. And this "self" is only a freedom, an absolute autonomy. This is what he intends to invent. This is the only value in an otherwise absurd world. And it is itself an absurdity. Man's project is doomed from the outset to frustration. For a man to be thus free is for him to be God. And this is absurdity squared. It is not only that man cannot be God. It is also that for a man to ex-sist God is for him not to ex-sist; for God does not ex-sist.

In the third place, the man of the Theater adheres to the myth of the death of God, but in his own sense. Unlike his modern predecessors, he has no will to disprove the existence of God. He does not even trouble himself, as they did, with proving that the traditional proofs do not prove. The quadriform medieval problematic—whether God is, what God is, how God is to be known, how God is to be named—has absolutely no meaning whatever for him. His question is biblical, whether God is here, now, with us. And his answer is negative.

To be exact, he does not say that God is dead, for this would be to imply that God once ex-sisted, that he once was-with-us. In one mood, the man of the Theater speaks of God's "missingness" (*der Fehl Gottes*). This is his mood of guilt and fear. The fear is that God may not be missing; perhaps he is only being missed when he is really here. The guilt lies in the feeling that

God is missing only because he has been dismissed. In another mood of more firm atheist purpose, however, the man of the Theater says that God is absent. And he says more than this when his post-modern intention is fully fixed. He says that God must be absent. He asserts his fundamental will that God should be absent. The reason is obvious. If God is present in the midst of men, man is dispossessed of the freedom toward which the will of the man of the Theater has set. If God is present, man is being made by God, and he is being made a man, a being with an essence and a nature. Therefore man is not free to make himself *ex nihilo,* out of a nothingness of nature and essence. If God is present, man's existence, which actualizes an essence, is transformed into a destiny, a destiny which he himself did not choose. A higher power of appointment, vested in the Pantokrator, is brought to bear on man, and under the weight of it his power to invent himself is crushed to nothingness. If God is present, if he is thus engaged as the higher Freedom in man's historical existence, man cannot exist. The living God is the death of man.

Therefore God must be declared dead, missing, absent. The declaration is an act of the will, a basic will to the absence of God. Like the post-modern man in the Marxist tradition, the man of the Theater is fundamentally God-opposed. However, he does not will, with Marx, the suppression of God from history. If he understands history at all, which is not the case, he could not understand it as Marx did. You would more exactly characterize his will if you were to reach for the biblical notion of "forgetting" God and if you were to understand it in a Freudian sense, which is indeed the sense of the Bible. The will of the man of the Theater thus becomes a will to the repression of God from consciousness. His project is to put God out of his conscious mind while God is still in his deep mind. Whatever your theological view of the matter, you must admit that the project entails a serious psychological risk.

The man of the Theater is, I said, an elusive figure, ill-defined even by himself, resisting definition by anyone else. At least he is a new figure, not to be disregarded even by us here in America. To us he may seem to be an alien figure only because we still live, or think we live, in the modern age and because the problem of evil has hitherto touched this blessed country only lightly. All the more should we attend to him; for there he stands as a judgment on the modern age. After all, the world that he declares to be absurd, the human existence from which he says that God is absent, the freedom of man that he sees as no more than a frustration—all these were the creations of modernity. If he is obsessed with the problem of evil, it is because this ancient problem in a newly complex and visible form was his heritage from modernity.

It is difficult to judge him, who is himself a judge. But if the judgment were to be drawn from some biblical source, I think the source would be the Book of Wisdom. It would be necessary, however, to alter the text somewhat. The Sage of Israel never met this kind of man in Egyptian Alexandria, then the cultural capital of the civilized world, where all sorts of men argued the problem of God. If the Sage had met our post-modern man of the Theater, he might well have written thus in judgment on him: "This man merits a lesser blame. It may be that he but goes astray in his search for God and in the will to find him. Absorbed in the human situation, he tries to fathom it. And he lets himself get caught in outward appearances, so dreadful are the things he sees." It is the other, ancient excuse (cf. Wisdom 13:6–7), the better excuse, that is still not an excuse.

It is time for me to bring to a conclusion this lengthy, but still too brief, analysis of the problem of God, yesterday and today. At least one conclusion is warranted. It has two parts.

First, it may be maintained with some justice that the modern problem of God, as raised by the godless man of the Academy, had a measure of diminishing continuity with the medieval problem as structured by Aquinas. Both problems were argued somehow in the same terms—existence and essence, knowledge and language. And for the disputants, the School and the Academy, the central question was the same—what God is. The issue was the intelligibility of God, as allied with the issue of the intelligibility of the world. In the post-modern age, however, this issue has become meaningless. If God is dead, as the post-modern postulate has it, why argue whether he be intelligible? Why argue whether the world be intelligible? Why, indeed, argue at all? The thing to do is one of two things—either change the world in the name of man's freedom to do so; or simply ex-sist the world in the name of man's freedom to do nothing else.

Second, in the post-modern age the problem of God has come back in its biblical mode of position. I should not say that it has come back. I should say rather that it has come up from the depths where it always is—from the depths of history that lie far below the level of day-to-day events, and from the depths of man's heart that lie far below the level of his day-to-day thoughts. The problem of God today is not posited simply in the order of ideas and affirmation where the terms of argument are essence and existence. Its plane of position is the historical-existential order, where the terms of argument are presence or transparency and absence or opacity. This is the plane on which the problem was posited by the Lord God of Israel when he visited and redeemed his people. This, too, is the plane on which it has again been posited by the man of the

Revolution and by the man of the Theater, who have come to visit, if not to redeem, us.

We who say we believe in God have some reason to be grateful to these men, the heirs of modernity, who have managed to better modernity's instruction. They have done us the service of bringing to the surface, so that it is all but palpable, our own problem, the religious problem, the human problem. They have stated the issue with rather appalling clarity, in a phrase calculated to shock us into awareness of its urgency. They have said that God is dead. So the affirmations clash. For we say that God is living.

The issue is drawn. Which is the myth and which is the reality? Is the myth in Nietzsche or in the New Testament? Is it in Marx or in Moses? Is it in Sartre of Paris or in Paul of Tarsus? Is God dead, as the prophet of the post-modern age proclaimed, or is he still the living God of more ancient prophecy, immortal in his being as He Who Is, deathlessly faithful to his promise to be with us all the days, even to the end of the epoch within which both the modern and the post-modern ages represent only moments in a longer dialectic of history?

I might transpose the statement of the issue into an idiom that is at once contemporary and also reminiscently biblical. Is the presence of God constitutive of man's historical existence or destructive of it? In order that a man may exist, "stand forth" as a man in freedom and in human action, what is required—that he recognize and acknowledge the presence of God, as the Old and New Testaments say, or that he ignore and refuse God's presence, as the Revolution and the Theater say? In order that the people may exist, organized for action in history as a force to achieve an historical destiny, what is required—that they disown God or own themselves to be his people? What is it that alienates man from himself—the confession of God's presence in history and in man's consciousness or the suppression of him from history and the repression of him from consciousness? How is it that a man or a people comes to desist, to "stand down" from human and civilized rank, to fall away into absurdity and non-existence—through knowledge of God or through ignorance of him?